WITHDRAWN-UNL

D1117846

MANAGING DEVELOPMENT THROUGH PUBLIC/PRIVATE NEGOTIATIONS

Rachelle L. Levitt
John J. Kirlin

Editors

ULI Project Staff

Rachelle L. Levitt, Director of Education, Project Manager
Frank H. Spink, Jr., Director of Publications
Robert L. Helms, Staff Vice President, Operations
Barbara M. Fishel/Editech, Manuscript Editor
M. Elizabeth Van Buskirk, Art Director
Christopher J. Dominiski, Artist
Tawanda R. Queen, Word Processing Specialist
Kathy Price, Word Processing
Louise E. Gant, Word Processing

Recommended bibliographic listing:

Levitt, Rachelle L., and Kirlin, John J., eds. Managing Development through Public/Private Negotiations. Washington, D.C.: ULI-the Urban Land Institute and the American Bar Association, 1985.

ULI Catalog Number M21
Library of Congress Catalog Number 85-51328
International Standard Book Number 0-87420-642-1

Copyright 1985 by ULI-the Urban Land Institute, 1090 Vermont Avenue, N.W., Washington, D.C. 20005, and the American Bar Association, 750 North Lake Shore Drive, Chicago, Illinois 60615.

Printed in the United States of America. All rights reserved. No part of this book may be reproduced in any form or by any means, electronic or mechanical, including photocopying, recording, or by any information storage or retrieval system, without permission of the publishers.

The opinions expressed in this publication are the authors' and are not to be construed to be those of ULI or the ABA.

About ULI

ULI-the Urban Land Institute is an independent, nonprofit educational and research organization that, from its incorporation in 1936, has been dedicated to improving the quality of land use planning and development and creating an atmosphere within which reasonable approaches to problem solving will prevail. ULI believes that these objectives can be achieved by conducting practical research to establish creditable information and by using education to communicate this information to public and private professionals in the many disciplines active in land use and development.

James A. Cloar
Executive Vice President
Urban Land Institute

About the ABA's Section of Urban, State, and Local Government Law

The American Bar Association was founded in 1878. Members of the ABA are attorneys in good standing at the bar of any state and the District of Columbia. Current membership numbers approximately 310,000. The ABA Section of Urban, State, and Local Government Law provides a common meeting ground and impartial forum for those members of the bar who deal with problems of urban, state, and local government, whether as attorneys for units of urban, state, or local government, as attorneys in private practice, as law teachers, or as students. The section furthers a better understanding of the law through holding meetings, undertaking studies, surveys, and analyses, publishing books, and disseminating current information concerning legislative and judicial decisions.

Lawrence J. Aurbach
Chairman, ABA Section of Urban,
State, and Local Government Law

iii

Editors

John J. Kirlin is professor of public administration at the Sacramento Public Affairs Center, University of Southern California. He specializes in public finance and public policy and has written numerous books and articles on the subjects.

Rachelle L. Levitt is director of education at the Urban Land Institute and specializes in various aspects of public/private partnerships.

Reviewers

Anita Miller
Assistant Attorney General
State of New Mexico
Sante Fe, New Mexico

Richard Carlisle
Partner
Freilich, Leitner & Carlisle
Kansas City, Missouri

Acknowledgments

This book is a collection of papers written by experts in negotiation, and it would not be possible without the efforts of numerous people, including of course the review committee and the contributing authors. Special thanks are due as well to Edward Abramson of the New York law firm Herrick, Freinstein for his help in preparing Chapter 2, "Public/Private Partnerships in Large-Scale Development Projects."

Rachelle Levitt, director of education at ULI, acted as project manager and co-editor of the book. John Kirlin, professor of public administration at the Sacramento Public Affairs Center of the University of Southern California, co-edited the book.

Special thanks are also due to Louise E. Gant, Tawanda Queen and Kathy Price for their patience and word processing skills.

CONTENTS

Foreword

Negotiations between public and private entities are increasingly being employed to reach agreements and secure approvals for development projects. The flexible zoning and growth management being adopted by many jurisdictions require negotiations as part of development review. Similarly, public/private joint ventures necessitate substantial negotiations and frequently complicated agreements. And in many cities and suburbs, large, complex projects are approved only after protracted bargaining with neighborhood and special interest groups and with public officials. Recognizing this important trend, the American Bar Association's Section of Urban, State, and Local Government Law and the Urban Land Institute held a seminar on the subject February 25-26, 1985, bringing together noted practitioners in the art of negotiating development approvals.

This publication is an outgrowth of that seminar; it includes papers and outlines written by the speakers at the ULI-ABA seminar and is a compilation of the latest thoughts about how negotiation can be accomplished and what legal constraints negotiators might face.

The seminar and this book represent an ongoing relationship between the ABA's Section on Urban, State, and Local Government Law and ULI's education and research program, and we are pleased to offer this joint publication. Further annual seminars and publications on topics of mutual concern can be expected.

Rachelle L. Levitt
Director of Education
Urban Land Institute

SECTION 1

OVERVIEW

Chapter 1

THE BARGAINING PROCESS: TRENDS AND ISSUES
John J. Kirlin

Bargaining between the public and private sectors is clearly increasing, and it is clearly affecting the development process. While some consider public/private bargaining an undesirable but inevitable phenomenon of the times, it is also an opportunity for the public and private sectors to achieve outcomes that they could not achieve alone. Both sides can profit, as illustrated by the most successful examples of bargaining between developers and local governments.

Bargaining Defined

The language used to discuss bargaining is important in how bargaining is perceived and valued. Bargaining is case-specific land use policy making that benefits both the public and private sectors. It involves agreeing to do something with and for each other in the context of a specific development. This definition contrasts with "rule application," where the public sector applies some set of already-established policies, such as a zoning ordinance, to a proposed development. In rule application processes, the developer proposes a specific land use plan to the public body, which judges its acceptability based on conformity to existing policies. The image is that of an almost mechanical, nondiscretionary judgment by the public sector--a litmus paper test. The public sector in this model is essentially passive: the developer proposes and the jurisdiction disposes. The public authority does not, however, seek to influence individual proposals. Its guidance

John J. Kirlin is professor of public administration at the Sacramento Public Affairs Center, University of Southern California, specializing in public finance and public policy.

of land uses is assumed to be exercised in the establishment of general policies, such as planning or zoning ordinances.

That image dominates the old, prebargaining system of land use policy making and development. It never accurately described the actual operations of the old system except in simple development projects, however. Nevertheless, it is a very powerful image. Developers, public officials, and citizens still often think of development approval as rule application. Rule application and bargaining constitute different processes. Rules are not irrelevant, but bargaining is not a rule application process.

It is useful to consider the effect of bargaining on taxes, fees, and exactions. Taxes and fees, two traditional ways of generating revenue for the public sector are applied uniformly to an asset or activity. As bargaining is case-specific, any revenues for the public sector (or public benefits provided to the developer) need not be uniform across cases. Further, the term "exaction" suggests force and one-directional flows of benefits. If participants approach bargaining as an occasion to exact what they seek, they are likely to miss opportunities to achieve benefits for both parties.

The Context for Bargaining

One factor that encourages bargaining is clearly fiscal constraint upon the public sector. Although California often comes first to mind in a discussion of fiscal constraint (primarily because of Proposition 13 in 1978), some 30 states now have a form of explicit limits upon the local or state fiscal resources available. Moreover, grants from the federal government, including those for sewer and road systems, important to many developments, are declining. Fiscal constraint is widespread and unlikely to ease. Because not enough public funds are available to support the infrastructure required for new development, public authorities turn to the developer proposing a project as a source of funds. In other cases, the local government sees opportunities to obtain funding for desired public works not clearly related to a particular development or even to secure revenues for other general purposes, such as the delivery of services.

The changing structure of our economy encourages bargaining. Agriculture continues to decline as a source of jobs. Manufacturing also represents a declining proportion of economic activity and employment. Equally important, the growing sectors of manufacturing (such as electronics) do not require the access to rail or water transportation important to earlier forms of manufacturing. They may locate outside existing concentrations of manufacturing. The most rapidly growing sector of the economy is the tertiary sector--services, retail trade, government, and finance, insurance, and real estate. Like the newer forms of manufacturing, such firms enjoy relatively wide latitude in choosing location. One consequence of these shifts in the economy is that jobs are increasingly being shifted out of central business districts. Indeed, by the Census Bureau's definition, more jobs are now being created in "suburban" locations than in "central cities."

The changing nature of employment and the wider latitude in choosing location place two new demands upon the public sector. Because employment is neither concentrated in location nor similar in technologies used, more particular demands regarding public works and services are placed upon the public sector. No longer is it feasible to support most of the economic activity in an area with a few focused major public works--a port, a railway system, or even freeways. Further, as large developments move into suburban locations, they are often being introduced into an existing residential setting. Available public works, scaled to residential land uses, may not be adequate for the new development. Upgrading and expanding public works in already populated areas is commonly more costly than for new developments. And current residents are commonly unwilling to bear the burden of the new infrastructure. Those proposing the new development are often the source of the needed funds. Moreover, the effects of increased development usually extend beyond public works to the environment and quality of life. They are also a subject of bargaining with developers.

These changes in the structure of the economy are strong forces. They encourage public/private bargaining for new development, and they do so independently of the fiscal condition of the jurisdiction where they are located. Bargaining will continue, even in the unlikely eventuality of a plumper public fisc.

However strong the forces encouraging bargaining, however, bargaining does not replace planning, zoning, and other instruments of land use policy. It builds on top of those established processes. Indeed, bargaining must draw much of its political legitimacy and legal defensibility from the traditional instruments of land use policy.

Bargaining neither wholly replaces taxes and fees as sources of public revenues nor destroys the need for traditional sources of public works funding--appropriations from the general funds, public debt, and intergovernmental grants, for example. Similarly, bargaining does not destroy whatever guarantees exist against the taking of private property or does not change the legal basis of vesting in a jurisdiction. Bargaining commonly adds to rather than substitutes for these traditional processes. And some of the most important constraints upon bargaining are found in these already established processes.

Where does bargaining occur? No systematic data are available on bargaining. No published data series records the bargains that are struck, their dollar value, or what each party to the bargain gave and received. Some anecdotal information is available, however.

Bargaining is the primary way public works are provided in California. Not nearly enough money is available through the traditional devices like bonds, grants, and general fund appropriations to provide the public works required by the amount of development that is occurring. The variety and amount of bargained-for public works is impressive. In one large case, a developer is providing up to $80 million for public works that at one time would have come from the public sector. The California Transportation Commission has adopted a policy effectively barring the expenditure of state and federal highway funds for construction of freeway interchanges to serve new development; they will now be the responsibility of affected local governments and developers. Bargaining is taking place not only in large mixed-use developments but also in more modest projects. Bargaining is endemic in California development, affecting all sorts of projects.

While the discussion thus far has emphasized public works, that vision of bargaining is too restrictive; many issues are brought into the process. An illustrative--but by no means exhaustive--list would include public works, land acquisition, land use zoning and other regulations, transportation impacts and systems, environmental impacts and mitigation strategies, housing (especially low and moderate income), employment patterns, fiscal relations, including equity partnerships, the provision of services, and maintenance and operation of facilities. Bargaining takes place in legally defined arenas, but it is not wholly constrained legally. While the law is important, bargaining ought not to be conceptualized merely in legal terms. It is of course risky and inadvisable for either sector to engage in something illegal. But the law is only an instrument of bargaining, not its real foundation. If the issues were simply legal, the resolution would be more commonly litigation than bargaining.

The real spur to bargaining is shared interest between the public and private sectors. Bargains should provide for shared interests, usually economic, between the developer and the jurisdiction. The bargaining process should be conducted with careful attention to legal requirements regarding hearings, public notice, established powers, and so forth, and the ultimate bargain is commonly recorded in legal documents, such as a development agreement or conditional zoning approval. (For more details, see Section 4 on conditional zoning approvals.) But the incentives to bargain and then to implement the agreement that arises from that bargained agreement should not be solely, or even predominantly, legal. The incentives should be found in shared interests.

The most important effects legal considerations have upon bargaining are defining the arenas where bargaining occurs, delimiting the issues to be included in bargaining and the language to be used, and providing the powers brought to the bargaining process by the public sector. (See Section 5 for an examination of the legal issues and constraints.) In California, for example, the following legally circumscribed arenas for bargaining have been defined: subdivisions, annexations, environmental impact assessments, specific plans, development agreements, zoning and building code administration, growth management systems, redevelopment, special districts, and assessment districts.

The Effects of Bargaining on the Development Process

Bargaining has definite effects upon the development process. The most important, but sometimes overlooked, is the opportunity to create more value for both sectors than could be created in the absence of bargaining. Bargaining need not be a game in which gains for the public sector are losses for the developer or vice versa.

As an example, consider the case of Solano Mall, a regional shopping center in Fairfield, California. One of the nation's largest shopping center developers several years ago approached the city, which lies in the growth path between San Francisco and Sacramento, and was urged to build a larger center than originally proposed. The city used its powers aggressively to make a larger center possible: it acquired land under

5

redevelopment authority, solved a drainage problem, moved an elementary school, constructed major improvements to adjacent streets, and obtained special state legislation allowing it to construct a freeway off-ramp to serve the project. The developer contributed to these activities by paying into an assessment district for the drainage system and by paying the city $1 million more than its land acquisition costs. The city also bargained for, and received, a junior equity position in the development, providing it a scaled share in gross rents and the proceeds of any sale or refinancing of the project. The first phases of the project have now been open nearly two years and are successful. Both the public and private sectors have benefited.

Bargaining also imposes new risks--economic and political--upon both developers and local governments. Consider first the public sector. If it is expecting bargaining with proponents of new development to provide a portion of the funds needed for future public works or the equity position that will allow them to fund the police department, these assumptions are clearly more risky economically than in the old system of relying upon tax revenues. They also commonly incur the increased political risks of being charged with having given too much to a developer (a charge difficult to counter when no standards have been established as to what is appropriate) or of being accountable when some development inevitably fails, placing in jeopardy the public benefits obtained through bargaining.

The developer also experiences greater risks, which arise from three factors: longer lead times from project conception to approval to allow for bargaining; additional interests (neighbors, for example) coming into the bargaining arena; and the common effect of requiring larger outlays before the project is approved (for special studies or just to participate in the bargaining). Interest rates or other project costs or the demand for space can increase dramatically during the extra time needed to bargain for project approval. An election or a new legal ruling can change the context of decision making quickly.

Bargaining also puts downward pressure on land prices. Any costs shifted from the public to the private sector must be borne by some individual(s), with the primary candidates being the developer, the ultimate users of the project, or the landowner from whom the developer purchases the land. As developers incorporate the expectation of bargaining and the likelihood of increased expenditures into their pro formas, they are likely to resist reducing their profit margins and to be wary of expecting to recapture increased costs through higher rents or selling prices. Where possible, they will seek to acquire land at lower costs. While this issue has not been systematically analyzed, such a shift of the costs to landowners appears to be occurring in some California jurisdictions.

New skills are needed, mostly in political and economic analysis and techniques of negotiation. On the public side, those involved must be skilled in the finance of development and in new instruments of public debt. Knowledge of the developer's probable pro forma for a project and of the constraints developers face from lenders and in marketing their project will allow public officials to approach bargaining effectively. Knowledge of tax increment financing, certificates of participation, and revenue bonds (among other public finance techniques) will afford greater opportunities for flexible structuring of the public/private partnership.

Developers, on the other hand, need to understand the finances and politics of the jurisdictions where they operate. Some of the knowledge required is specific: developers must know about specific personalities, about campaign finance, about the groups active in land use politics, and about any conflict concerning the area where the project is located. In addition, developers need more general knowledge of public finance and politics.

Negotiation skills are commonly required. But the issue is not just skills narrowly defined as possessed by individuals. Equally important is establishing expectations and procedures that support bargaining and allow time for successful negotiation to occur.

Key Issues Raised by Bargaining

The growing practice of public/private bargaining raises four key issues:

o   striking acceptable, enduring bargains
o   satisfying norms of equity and political legitimacy
o   ensuring political accountability
o   creating value for both the public and private sectors.

Striking an acceptable, enduring bargain is the presumed goal of both the developer and the public entity. Complex, large development projects can extend for nearly a decade from inception to completion;

7

even smaller projects can extend over several years. Both public and private parties must achieve a stable base of expectations so the process can be acceptably concluded and can last through the long implementation phase.

To achieve the goal, both sides must avoid false starts, overexpectations, unrealistic promises, and surprises. They must bargain realistically and in good faith. Each side must represent its interests, but it must do so recognizing that meeting the other party's interests is critical to success. Value must be created for all parties to the negotiation.

Further, each party must identify and to the extent possible control the arenas where bargaining takes place. One of the dilemmas in public/private bargaining is "arena management." The earlier lists of legally based arenas and of possible issues provide some clues as to the variations possible in arenas. If the arenas keep shifting, it is hard for the parties to stabilize their relationship and the elements of the bargain. Each arena invokes additional participants, new legal and procedural issues, and new languages in which to conduct the dialogue. Controlling the arenas is very difficult. A neighborhood group might challenge the bargain in court on environmental grounds, for example, which creates a new arena. Or some member(s) of the state legislature might decide that an issue requires their scrutiny and intervention, and suddenly the action shifts to hearings and votes in a legislative committee. At a minimum, the most likely arenas where bargaining will occur must be identified and their interaction and relationships understood so that a path can be charted.

One of the possible results of moving from arena to arena is "death by a thousand nicks." In each arena, the parties might reach an agreement that makes sense at that point, but added to other agreements, the project becomes unworkable. Avoiding this fate and moving forward expeditiously are the primary objectives of arena management. While it is easy to imagine the sequential nicks affecting the developer's bottom line in a project, the same dynamics can make a project unworkable for public authorities. Imagine a scenario in which negotiations are underway and it is understood what the developer wants. Suppose a few months later the developer returns to say his reading of the market has changed and that light industrial facilities rather than office buildings are required--all of which means that the requirements for public works have also changed.

Once the bargain is struck and an agreement has been reached, attention shifts to implementing it and ensuring compliance with its provisions. At this point, legally enforceable documents must be drafted concerning the implementation of the agreement--but the necessity of having to use them must be avoided. The best way to accomplish this task is to structure the bargain so that both sides benefit; thus, both sides have a stake in ensuring the bargain's implementation.

Norms of equity and political legitimacy must be satisfied. A major challenge encountered in bargaining arises from the common definition of equity as treating "equal cases equally." The same test is often used to infer political legitimacy, as in "the system is legitimate because it treats everyone equally." But public/private bargains concerning new development require specific decisions. It is hard to decide which cases are "equal" and what equal treatment would involve. The public sector might exert pressure to compare development proposals, seeking equivalence in treatment: "This proposal is like one we did with x three months ago, so that is what we should do this time." Similarly, a developer may know what sort of bargain was struck on a similar proposal a year ago and expect identical treatment.

These expectations are not unreasonable. But they cannot be met in the context of bargaining. Bargaining depends on the specific case. If it does not, taxes or fees will be imposed or development approvals issued on the basis of established policies. Established policies can be uniform, treating equal cases equally, but bargaining cannot. Thus, while an examination of previous cases might provide guidance concerning the bargain that is probable in the case under negotiation, it will not produce an exact solution.

The difficulty is that the wish to identify equal cases and treat them equally is deeply ingrained in our culture. Not only public/private bargaining challenges this norm, however. Are equal cases being treated equally when entrants into today's housing market face higher real prices and interest rates than those of two decades ago? The treatment of the two different age groups that entered the market at different times might be considered equal, but it is not equal treatment of first-time homebuyers.

Other standards of equity and legitimacy thus need to be developed and used in the bargaining process. Three alternatives exist:

o   Equitable processes, usually defined as affording access of all affected individuals and groups (stakeholders) to participate in decision making; while representatives (for example, city councils) may still be the decision makers, all who wish to should have the opportunity to provide input;

o   Equitable outcomes, where the results of the bargaining process are judged equitable and legitimate (for example, the public as a whole benefits and costs and benefits are distributed appropriately among individuals and groups);

o   Predictability, where the assumption is that if the rules of the game are well known and stable, individuals and firms can adjust their behaviors to those rules.

Bargaining can meet these concepts of equity and legitimacy more readily than it can the standard of equal cases treated equally. Where possible, policy processes and dialogue should be moved in the direction of using these alternative norms.

Ensuring political accountability is the third key issue confronted as public/private bargaining becomes more commonplace. At one level, the issue is linguistic: how to have bargaining perceived as an appropriate exercise of political decision making and not as inappropriate "zoning for sale" or other labels suggesting that public officials are not being accountable to citizens and are instead pursuing their own interests. At another level, the issue is structural: because many of the mechanisms designed to ensure accountability focus on the establishment of uniform policies (hearing requirements for adoption of a general plan, for example), they may not work in the context of requirements for specific cases required of bargaining.

The remedies for both the linguistic and the structural dimensions of political accountability are the same: to prepare politically, organizationally, and legally for bargaining. Explicit preparations for bargaining should be made part of the jurisdiction's "routine" policy making. They might include, for example, identification of public works that can be partially financed from the developer's contributions in a capital budget, provision of density bonuses, and development of more detailed planning documents (specific plans or master environmental impact studies, for example) for areas of special interest to developers and the jurisdiction. At the organizational level, a bargaining team can be identified (it might, for example, include the city manager, finance director, planning director, public works director, and city attorney) and procedures established by which bargaining takes place. In all of these efforts, the intent is to prepare the setting for bargaining. The public and the press will have been exposed to the idea. Public officials, elected and appointed, will have a framework within which to approach bargaining and from which to explain their actions to constituents.

Preparation for bargaining both constrains and empowers public participants. Preparation should constrain in largely desirable ways, by setting objectives and identifying possible tradeoffs among them. If objectives are unrealistic, they could paralyze the process and preclude the needed flexibility. Preparation can also make the bargaining process expected rather than surprising, can provide policy guidance, and can provide important defenses against attacks upon the legality and appropriateness of bargaining. The last point is especially important. The strongest political and legal defenses of bargaining are that it occurs in a well-prepared context where public participation has been widespread and effective and where the public interest has been well served.

Creating value for both the private and public sectors is the key to successful bargaining. An important starting point for bargaining is understanding each other's constraints. Public participation is an absolute constraint in the public sector, for example. No complex bargain can be completed without public hearings, votes of public officials or citizens, and, often, the media's scrutiny of both developer and public officials. For the developer, prevalent ratios of financial institutions (debt coverage) and market forces (interest rates or rental prices) are equally compelling. As no bargaining can be successful if these constraints are violated, no value can be created for either the public or private sectors unless they are respected.

Bargaining can create value that cannot be created by either the public or private sector acting independently. While so apparent as to be commonplace, a commitment to achieving this result is often missing. One reason is found in the stylized images of separate--even hostile-- public and private sectors existing in our culture. The image of the private sector as creator of growth, employment, and wealth, virtually despite the public sector, still exists. Similarly, the image of the public sector as protector of the public interest against the ravages of rapacious private interests also exists. These images hinder recognition of the interdependence of the two sectors and of the opportunities to satisfy the public interest through economic growth.

Conclusion

The issue of negotiation is especially pressing at this time in our nation's history. As the economy continues to change from the primary and secondary sectors toward the tertiary sector, the demands for new jobs are very large. Six to 8 percent of existing jobs are lost every year. Combined with the natural increases in the population and labor force, these losses mean that the nation must create as many new jobs about every 15 years as now exist. Many of these jobs are at new locations; the closed steel plant is not the location of the new financial services office or electronics assembly plant. Even if replacement jobs are created in the same city or region, new development is required. And new development often requires different land uses. New development also often requires new public works, new services, and even new governmental authorities (new cities or new special districts, for example). Only by acting together, using the powers of both the private and public sectors, can these challenges be met.

Making successful bargaining routine rather than exceptional is critical to the future of our nation. While one theme of this chapter, illustrated in the following chapters, is that bargaining in the context of new development is widespread, it is not routine. Land use policy making and development are still captured by the procedures of the past. Most developers' pro formas and time schedules do not provide adequate recognition of the public/private negotiation that proposed projects are likely to encounter. And much public policy making still proceeds as if the public sector had the capacity to achieve its policy goals with its own resources. Making successful bargaining routine rather than exceptional will require new attitudes, new skills, new organizational designs, and new policies. Clear goals, strategic policies, flexible organizational structures, and the ability to negotiate and to mobilize resources are needed. These changes will be required of both governments and developers. They can succeed in the future only through joint action, and they are likely to become more similar: the private sector more attentive to accommodation of varied interests and the public sector more entrepreneurial.

SECTION 2

TECHNIQUES IN NEGOTIATING PUBLIC/PRIVATE AGREEMENTS

Real estate projects are increasingly being developed under specific written agreements between public and private entities when joint projects are conceived and the various interests exhibit significant concern. These agreements take many forms, but the common thread is the need to develop a process that brings discordant groups together. Section 2 examines these forms of agreements and provides specific examples of the process used to come to agreement.

Robert Freilich, in "Public/Private Partnerships in Large-Scale Development Projects," examines the expanding and changing roles of the public and private sectors. The chapter discusses the sectors' competing objectives, how they can be brought together to achieve mutually beneficial ends, and the ultimate agreement.

Negotiation techniques and strategies in public/private projects from the public sector's point of view are described by Richard Fosmoen in "The Public Sector's Perspective." Providing practical advice to negotiators representing the public interest, this paper describes the major tenets essential to negotiation, including how to define the city's objectives and how to involve the essential players.

Lindell Marsh, in "Focal Point Planning in Key Largo, Florida," describes a negotiation process that can be used to bring together varied interests with apparently irreconcilable differences to form an agreement that will be satisfactory to all concerned. The case presented is an environmental issue in Key Largo, Florida.

In "A Public Official's Experience with Public/Private Development: Battery Park City," Barry Light describes the intense negotiation process that occurred in selecting a developer for the commercial and residential components of Battery Park City, New York.

The negotiation process for the Austin Republic Square District is described in "Stakeholders Analysis Applied to the Republic Square District," by Michael Buckley. Stakeholders analysis provides a useful tool for formulating a development strategy for an area and developing a basis for negotiating between the many actors that become involved in development.

Chapter 2

PUBLIC/PRIVATE PARTNERSHIPS IN LARGE-SCALE DEVELOPMENT PROJECTS
Robert H. Freilich

The provision of public infrastructure by the private sector and the concept of public/private partnership are creatures of the 1980s necessitated by fiscal austerity at all levels of government. The 1970s saw rapid growth that emphasized regulatory land issues, such as exclusionary zoning (the accommodation of low- and moderate-income housing), growth management (the accommodation of growth tied to adequate public facilities and capital improvement programming),[1] and environmental impact. In periods of rapid growth, government's role is primarily that of regulator, to prevent societal problems from occurring as a result of too-rapid expansion of the private sector.[2] The 1980s, in contrast, have focused on retrenchment, highlighted by the new federalism, civil rights, inverse condemnation and antitrust liability, limitations on state taxes and expenditures, budget cuts, and the elimination of federal grant and loan programs traditionally employed to finance redevelopment of the urban core and the extension of infrastructure to the urban fringe.

One can see most effectively the changing roles of the public and private sectors in downtowns and in existing urban neighborhoods. Traditionally, the public sector was involved in development, if at all, through urban renewal in central cities. Even in that pursuit, the role of the government was completely separated from that of the private redeveloper, who purchased the land after the city had acquired it, cleared it, and readied it for redevelopment. The city's role in urban renewal was to eliminate blight and deterioration in central cities and to use grants and other funds as incentives to stimulate the process of distributing land to developers.

Robert Freilich is Hulen Professor of Law in Urban Affairs at the University of Missouri-Kansas City School of Law. He is a partner in the law firm of Freilich, Leitner & Carlisle in Kansas City, Missouri, which has worked extensively in public/private partnership projects.

These separate roles were not without problems: the city's forecast for future growth and its comprehensive master plan were not marketable to the private sector. In many cases, the private sector's involvement proved to be economically infeasible, because the public sector was investing large sums in providing infrastructure in the suburbs and the middle class was fleeing close-in city areas for the suburbs. That tide has turned, however, and with renewed private interest in downtown and existing neighborhoods, cities are now ready to use the large tracts of cleared, undeveloped land assembled earlier. Further, development by the private sector is now necessary because, since the Nixon years, federal programs have been greatly reduced. And the federal programs that are available, such as Urban Development Action Grants (UDAGs), require leveraging of both public and private funds, necessitating the private sector's involvement.

Opportunities for joint public/private projects are by no means limited to redevelopment. Government entities at all levels are finding innovative ways to increase revenues by participating in--in some instances initiating--private development projects. One area where public/private efforts have been particularly successful is in the financing of infrastructure and other public facilities that support private development projects. Cities and counties are joining with private developers to construct sports stadia, convention centers, and parking facilities. Urban mass transit authorities are participating as private partners in developing the areas around transit stations. Quasi-public institutions like universities and hospitals are participating with the private sector to develop research parks, hotels on university campuses, and medical office buildings within hospital complexes.[3] Clearly, public/private partnerships can be adapted for use in any number of situations.

The Roles of the Partners

In development projects, government no longer plays only the role of planner and grantsman. While it was once responsible for assembling a site, writing down the cost of acquisition and clearance, providing the infrastructure to serve the site, and establishing the municipal financing mechanisms for certain funding, such as tax-exempt bonds, it now has expanded its role. The new role includes sharing risks, participating in loan commitments and mortgages, sharing operating as well as capital costs, participating in sale/leaseback arrangements, reducing administrative red tape for the private sector, providing favorable tax-exempt financial packages, encouraging cooperation among municipal entities, and creating special redevelopment authorities.

The role of the private sector has been expanded as well to include the developer's participation in planning, designing, financing, and, ultimately, marketing the project. The private developer's contributions to a public/private partnership are the furnishing of risk capital, his practical experience, his expertise in economics, imagination, energy, and optimism. The private sector has become involved in the financing, design, construction, ownership, and operation of the infrastructure and public facilities that serve the site, such as sewer, water, and electricity. In addition to declining federal resources, voters have limited city expenditures by approving such referenda as California's Proposition 13 in 1978 and Massachusetts's Proposition 2-1/2 in 1980. And it has become more common for the private sector to finance infrastructure by the city's imposition of development exactions and impact fees.

In two major decisions in California affecting the City of San Diego, J.W. Jones Co. v. City of San Diego, 157 Cal. App. 3d 745, 203 Cal. Rptr. 580 (1984), and City of San Diego v. Holodnak, 157 Cal. App. 3d 759, 203 Cal. Rptr. 797 (1984), both of which were denied hearing in the California Supreme Court on August 23, 1984, the California Court of Appeals upheld the most far-reaching ordinances in the United States for financing capital infrastructure on the suburban fringe. The ordinances implemented a 1979 General Plan in which the city was organized into three growth areas: the existing neighborhoods and downtown ("urbanized"), the developing fringe ("planned urbanizing"), and an area premature for development ("future urbanizing"). The planned urbanizing area was divided into thirteen planned community areas and through detailed capital improvement programs and financing plans, all improvements in the areas are paid for through "flexible benefit assessments" (FBAs) on development, a combination of police power impact fees and benefit assessments. Developments in the urbanizing area were exempt from these FBAs since services were already available. The FBAs were based upon the contribution of each unit of residential, commercial, and industrial development to traffic, park, library, school, fire, and other facility capacities. Combining a lien on the properties (special assessment) with payment postponed to the building permit stage

17

(police power), the system is also annually adjusted for inflationary cost increases. In 1983, four years after the plan was adopted, the city had a record building year of more than 16,000 building permits, and for the first time since World War II, more than 60 percent of new growth was occurring in the infill areas.

Impact fees also using the generation of need created by the development were approved in far-reaching opinions in Florida. Road impact fees were upheld in Home Builders & Contractors Assoc. v. Board of County Commissioners, 446 So.2d 140 (Fla. App. 1983), and countywide park fees in Hollywood, Inc. v. Broward County, 431 So.2d 606 (Fla. App. 1983).[4]

The private sector's participation in a partnership with a public entity is not without drawbacks. For instance, the earnings that the private developer may generate might be limited, and the private sector's autonomy is likely to be reduced. The partnership between the public and private sectors is therefore a delicate balance.

Competing Objectives

The public and private sectors have competing objectives for a joint project. The government's interests in and objectives for a project include:

o   revitalizing socially and economically depressed areas;

o   increasing the tax base of the redevelopment area;

o   improving the quality of life for citizens by providing schools, power stations, sewage facilities, roads, and parks;

o   providing jobs;

o   creating a public monument of aesthetic merit, without regard to economics;

o   minimizing the environmental impact of the project and its effect on the community and its neighborhoods;

o   ensuring compliance with its comprehensive plan, master lease, enabling legislation, and bond resolution; and

o   creating a profit center with which to seed future development.

The private sector has different objectives. Its primary objective is to maintain its reputation as a developer by meeting construction deadlines, making all scheduled monetary payments, and complying with the agreed-upon development plan. Second, the developer wants to negotiate a deal that yields the maximum return on investment. Last, he wants to satisfy the requirements established by his private institutional lenders and investors.

To ensure that both parties achieve their respective goals, several decisions must be incorporated into the agreement between the partners. The parties must decide who--public or private sector--will assume the lead role. Government entities must decide among themselves who will be the leader for the government, who will assemble the property and how transfers of land by sale or lease will be accomplished, how to raise funds to acquire and clear the land, who will provide the design guidelines, who will prepare the environmental impact studies, and who will develop the request for proposals (RFP).

Assuming that these early decisions are made primarily by the government, the private developer enters the picture by submitting a proposal in response to the RFP. Based on the aesthetic merit of the proposal, the developer's reputation, credit-worthiness, and affirmative action record, the economic benefits the government will receive as a result of the project, and the developer's interest in forging alliances with other developers if necessary (as was done in the Times Square project in New York City), the government must select the developer and award a conditional designation. Conditional designation should be based upon final architectural plans and firm financing commitments and letters of credit. The developer should understand the consequences of delays in the project, and per diem charges for delay should be included. The developer should further understand that default on a provision of a master development agreement may result as a matter of law in "dedesignation." Dedesignation is a Draconian measure; therefore, the criteria as to what behavior might result in dedesignation must be clearly established early and written into the development agreement. (As a practical matter, dedesignation may be very difficult because of

19

resulting delays, loss of momentum, and damage to the government's and the project's image.)

The parties then have more decisions: Who will provide infrastructure? Who will pay for it? Who will finance it? How will the site be transferred to the developer? The form of the transfer, either sale or lease, depends upon the developer's ability to finance the project, police the agreement, and share profits, and the importance of ultimate ownership. The resolution of all these issues must be included in an overall master agreement.

The Partnership Agreement

The partnership agreement is a written statement of the decisions governing all of the various aspects of the project. It provides adequate protection for bond holders, including obligations for rental payments and payments in lieu of taxes. It provides flexibility in establishing important federal income tax considerations and is critical in determining deductibility[5] for federal income taxes, especially in sale/leaseback arrangements. If property taxes are assessed on separate lots, new arrangements must be worked out with the assessor to accommodate the assembled or unified parcels. The partnership agreement establishes provisions for maintenance charges for public facilities. It establishes each party's share of the income stream, proceeds from mortgage refinancing, and proceeds from sales. The agreement establishes the time schedule for the project and requires timely commencement and completion of construction. The agreement's construction clause contains some type of security of the developer's obligations--personal guarantees, surety bonds, letters of credit, or other collateral. At the same time, the agreement must include some protection for the developer from defaults on the government's obligation to provide infrastructure and rent abatement, and it must require consequential damages in the event of the government's default. The agreement must contain provisions for quality control governing aesthetic judgments, interior and exterior design, and construction standards. If multiple developers are involved in a large-scale project, the partnership agreement must establish how to resolve any conflicts between developers. Finally--and perhaps most important--the written partnership agreement must not be too rigid. It must provide guidelines and set forth certain fundamental decisions, but it must be able to be amended and must not impede the development of the project.

Financing the Development

As the stream of federal funds traditionally used to finance development projects has slowed to a trickle, innovative and creative financing techniques have been developed, including tax-exempt financing and the issuance of municipal bonds (direct obligation, general obligation, special assessments, tax-increment financing, special districts, revenue bonds with general obligation backing, and industrial development bonds) for land acquisition, site improvements, and the construction of infrastructure and private facilities. Constitutional debt limitations must be provided for in the partnership agreement. Other creative financing techniques are available: sale/leaseback agreements, tax- exempt leases, or installment purchase contracts. While these techniques might appear extremely advantageous, the parties must carefully analyze the tax consequences of each, and the agreement must comply with all IRS requirements.[6]

Conclusion

A large-scale urban development project incorporating a public/private partnership is a complex endeavor. It is, however, the wave of the future, and lawyers and urban planners familiar with the process will certainly be in demand. These guidelines should be a useful framework for analyzing the roles of the various parties in the process.

Notes

[1] The issue of growth management is highlighted by <u>Golden</u> v. <u>Planning Board of Ramapo</u>, 30 N.Y.2d 359, 285 N.E.2d 291, 334 N.Y.S.2d 138, <u>appeal dismissed</u>, 409 U.S. 1003 (1972). See Robert Freilich and John Ragsdale, "Timing and Sequential Controls: The Essential Basis for Effective Regional Planning. An Analysis of the New Directions for Land Use Control in the Minneapolis-St. Paul Metropolitan Region," 58 <u>Minn. L. Rev.</u> 1009 (1974).

[2] For a complete analysis of the issues of the 1970s, see Robert Freilich and Eric O. Stuhler, <u>The Land Use Awakening: Zoning Law in the 70s</u> (Chicago: ABA Press, 1981).

[3] See Rachelle L. Levitt, ed., <u>Research Parks and Other Ventures: The University/Real Estate Connection</u> (Washington, D.C.: ULI-the Urban Land Institute, 1985) for a detailed discussion of this phenomenon.

[4] Robert Freilich and Gene Pal, <u>New Developments in Land Use and Environmental Regulations</u> (Institute on Planning, Zoning, and Eminent Domain, 1985), 1-1, 1-18 to 1-19.

[5] For an excellent discussion of the tax considerations and consequences of the various types of public/private agreements, see Quinn and Olstein, "Privatization: Public/Private Partnerships Providing Essential Services," 5 <u>Mun. Fin. J.</u> 247, 249 (1984).

[6] See Gary Stout and Joseph Vitt, <u>Public Incentives and Financing Techniques for Codevelopment</u> (Washington, D.C.: ULI-the Urban Land Institute, 1982) for a discussion of financing tools available to the public sector.

Chapter 3

THE PUBLIC SECTOR'S PERSPECTIVE
Richard L. Fosmoen

Negotiating complex public development deals requires part rough-hewn skill and part fine art, and public officials, professional staff, and developers involved in public/private negotiations should keep three major tenets foremost in their thinking: (1) to define clearly the public sector's objectives; (2) to always know who the players are and to keep them involved; and (3) to keep the negotiations as simple as possible, focusing on the business deal first and then implementing the legal document. These key elements should be the basis of any questions that anyone involved in the negotiations might ask. If these points are properly addressed at the beginning and kept clearly in mind throughout negotiations, it will make every job easier and ensure that the product--a successfully completed development project--has all the ingredients for which everybody bargained.

Although these points seem relatively simple and elementary, it is surprising how often public officials attempt to negotiate deals without keeping them in mind. Consequently, whether a relatively small neighborhood zoning case or a major mixed-use development with many layers of public and private financing, the deal often fails, the end product is unsatisfactory to the city and to the public, and the city's credibility in the eyes of elected officials, citizens, and developers suffers greatly.

Generally, city staff who negotiate with the private sector do not have any formal training in techniques of negotiation. Most city professionals are administrators, technicians, or planning and zoning officials who lack formal skills in negotiating and who learn on the job. The public sector still has a long way to go to educate its representatives about how to represent properly the city's best interests.

Richard Fosmoen is assistant city manager of the City of Miami Beach, Florida.

Define the City's Objectives

The first step for a public sector negotiator is to determine what the city wants to receive from negotiation--not an easy task. Public professionals often represent numerous client groups with varying interests and objectives. Each setting for negotiation is different, and each carries a different set of objectives. Furthermore, the public sector's objectives have been known to change in midstream.

The public sector negotiating team will be looking to achieve a variety of different objectives:

o   Quality design: Although often dictated by zoning and design guidelines, specialized design features can also be achieved through density bonuses, profitable but otherwise unallowed uses in the project, and other techniques.

o   Demands from citizen groups: Citizen groups typically try to alleviate the impact of a project on the current conditions of the area involved. Their concerns include parking, traffic, height, density, design, and physical and socioeconomic impact on the neighborhood.

o   Affirmative action: Inevitably it is extremely important to provide for affirmative action practices to meet the public's objectives and to develop broad community support for the project.

o   Infrastructure development: Large development projects typically require additional construction, expansion, and/or upgrading of streets, sewer and water capacity, and other public services. Although these functions traditionally are funded by public funds, today's fiscal climate and the recent history of federal cutbacks for such expenditures often require the private sector to share in providing these services.

o   Expansion of the tax base: One of the foremost objectives of the public sector for any development project is to expand the municipal tax base.

o   Elected officials: It is important to remember that mayors and city commissioners or councillors are elected by the people. Their support or endorsement of a successful development project is critical to their future political careers. Likewise, when projects they have endorsed do not succeed or are viewed as detrimental for the community, elected officials are devastated.

o   Financial resources: Although many public sector officials believe profit is a dirty word, in this age of dwindling fiscal resources, the potential for additional revenues for the public coffers from development should be foremost in the public negotiator's mind. Development deals that require public financing, the provision of infrastructure, zoning changes, many hours (even years) of city staff time, and numerous other concessions also require that the city share the project's potential profits.

It is important to remember that two types of negotiated development deals occur in two different climates for development. Either a developer initiates a project and approaches the city with a specific proposal, or the city initiates the project and seeks a developer to undertake it. When the city initiates the project, it has time to think out its objectives; usually, the objectives are clear and formally defined in a request for proposal or a specific plan outlining the city's development requests. When a developer approaches a city to initiate a development project, however, the public sector's reaction is generally best described as knee-jerk. Typically, the developer has thought through the process and what he wants out of the negotiations, but the city, responding quickly to the proposal, has to formulate its objectives as it goes. In such situations, the city negotiator must step back, collect his or her thoughts, and define the objectives before beginning the negotiations.

Further, a development deal is negotiated in varying development climates. Whether the market is weak or strong for the type of development being proposed affects what the city's objectives are and what negotiators are able to achieve from the negotiations. City negotiators must understand the development and investment climate that they are working with and plan their strategy for negotiation accordingly.

Know the Players

Development negotiators must understand all the participants who will negotiate the development deal. A whole cast of characters almost invariably becomes involved in one form or another before the contract is signed: the developer, city staff, elected officials, citizen groups, the media, state agencies, federal agencies, environmental groups, and various other interest groups. Each player has a different interest and a different agenda. Each group will provide input for the negotiated agreement, and each group has the power to approve a development agreement or to kill the deal.

Early in the process, the roles and the input that each organization will provide must be defined. City officials should first ask themselves whether they really want to deal with the developer. Is the city in a position to negotiate with the developer, is it willing to take certain risks, and is it flexible? These questions must be answered before negotiations begin.

Professional city staff should determine the members of the negotiating team and identify a leader who has the authority and the confidence of all the other players to make decisions and to deal with the press, the public, the developers, other staff, and other parties involved. This person must have authority and must have the confidence of everyone involved in the deal. The leader must direct the input from the numerous city departments and individuals and must have the capability to make command decisions when necessary. City staff must also define the roles that each member of the negotiating team will play. The city attorney should be involved in all aspects of the negotiations but usually is not the best person to negotiate the deal. It is often helpful to bring in an outside advisor to act as middleman between the city and the developer to mediate and negotiate difficult items. A third-party, impartial advisor can often break down intractable positions on both sides of the bargaining table and can negotiate compromises that appear nonnegotiable.

Elected officials must be kept informed of the process, but they need to be kept at arm's length until the appropriate time for their decision. Many states (Florida, for example) have strict sunshine laws that prevent officials' participating in negotiations unless all meetings are open to the public and the press. It is therefore difficult to involve elected officials in early stages of negotiation. Because elected officials are concerned about the status of negotiations and when the project will be built, however, it is critical to keep them informed throughout negotiations.

Citizen groups come in various sizes, shapes, forms, and conditions. The city negotiator must know what they want and, furthermore, what they are willing to settle for--often two extremely different items. The negotiator must tread a fine line to ensure that citizen groups feel they are participating but that their demands do not become so extreme so as to scare the developer off or ultimately to kill the deal.

The media are constantly curious about development deals. A misplaced story in the morning newspaper will negate months and months of negotiation. The negotiating team must select a leader to provide the media with information about the project. Again, the leader must tread a fine line between providing the media with premature information and concealing information that is public record.

Other interest groups and parties will spring up to become involved in the development deal. Federal, state, and environmental regulatory agencies often have power to review development projects. These agencies must be involved early during negotiations to understand their demands (see Chapter 9, "Negotiating in an Intergovernmental Context"). Often, cities and developers must unite after negotiation to advocate a project that a federal or state regulatory agency does not view favorably. A united front from the city and the developer often has more political clout in the governor's office or in Washington than does one party's attempt to change the agency's mind. It is impossible to predict when or which other interest groups and ad hoc organizations will spring up to challenge the project, but the city staff must be prepared to deal with these groups.

Keep It Simple

Negotiations leading to real estate development are complex. Every effort must be made to keep the negotiations and the arrangements as simple as possible. Potential development deals can die because cities are too inflexible. Not understanding how far the negotiation process can go can place too many demands on a real estate project.

Before entering negotiations, the public sector must ask itself whether the plan, the zoning, the sources of financing, and other conditions are flexible enough to withstand the give and take of negotiation. City officials should be willing to bend in negotiations. If they cannot take certain risks, they should not negotiate.

City negotiators must know basic real estate arithmetic. They must know the developer's absolute bottom line when negotiating for gross rents and percentages of income. (Development consultants can guide the development team to ensure that what the city is proposing is feasible.) Furthermore, knowing what is reasonable is important to ensure that negotiations proceed smoothly. Dade County officials, for example, negotiated a management agreement for the new Dade County government center that took almost two years to complete because the negotiating team had no knowledge of the industry's standard fees for management of retail facilities.

It is far more preferable to accept a smaller share of gross income than a share of net income. Too many costs can be buried in net income; further, some states do not allow municipalities to participate as a partner in a real estate deal. Most courts interpret sharing a portion of net income as participating as a partner, and, many cities consequently cannot accept net income.

Enforcing the development agreement is essential to ensure a project's timely completion. Cities must build "trigger points" into performance standards requiring the developer to proceed with the project. These formal trigger points will help ensure that the developer proceeds as agreed--that he does not hold the property while the city meets its requirements in the development agreement. Requiring the developer to exercise options, break ground, secure financing, and identify development schedules by a given date helps ensure that public improvements are made on an appropriately phased schedule as private development proceeds. The greatest leverage a city can bring to bear on a private developer is to force him to carry the costs of financing an uncompleted development project. If the city can require the developer to convert the option into an agreement to purchase land, take out a construction loan, or pay for putting steel in the ground before the city makes a series of costly improvements in infrastructure, then the city has the leverage to ensure that the private sector carries out the development agreement.

A final word of caution is necessary for the public sector: city officials must be able to meet their commitments. The process requires not only financial and administrative capability but also the political capacity to carry out the final development agreement.

Chapter 4

FOCAL POINT PLANNING IN KEY LARGO, FLORIDA
Lindell L. Marsh

As negotiation and bargaining become increasingly significant components of land use planning, historic planning processes are becoming outdated. Particularly for complex and regionally significant projects, new processes must be devised to provide a forum for the negotiation of issues raised by the local, state, and federal public and the private interests involved. "Focal point planning" and "habitat conservation planning" (a type of focal point planning), used for a recent development in Key Largo, Florida, are such processes.

Focal point planning, in contrast to comprehensive planning, focuses on a specific issue or issues, such as financing infrastructure or (in the case of North Key Largo--see Figure 1) the conservation of wildlife and development compatible with that conservation. Habitat conservation planning (HCP) is an experimental public/private sector process used to develop a plan for future land uses in the area that will resolve significant conflicts between public concerns for wildlife (in the case of Key Largo, several endangered species and unusual vegetative habitat) and private development. An essential part of the process is the provision of specific assurances to the various parties, normally in the form of an agreement that the plan will be honored. HCP is based on the assumption that this society is moving away from the principle that the governance of our land and natural resources is the primary role of the private developer and toward the principle that a number of public interests and agencies must share in the planning and management of these resources.

Key Largo is the first island off the tip of the Florida mainland, the gateway to the Florida keys. With the exception of the Ocean Reef Club, one of the most exclusive resorts on the East Coast, the northern 12 miles of the key are virtually undeveloped, probably because it is close to the Florida Everglades, a constant source of moist air, mosquitoes, and other animal life more common to a swamp or marsh.

Lindell Marsh is a partner in the law firm Nossaman Guthner Knox & Elliott, Costa Mesa, California.

In 1984, several major landowners became concerned that the proposed listing of two species, the wood rat and the cotton mouse, as endangered would severely limit their ability to develop their lands. Key Largo is also habitat for the only species of American crocodile (also listed as endangered) and is bordered by the John Pennekamp Coral Reef State Park, site of the only living coral reef in the continental United States--a horror chamber for developers. In this case, the 53 landowners were long-term investors and had no choice but to attempt to find a way out.

The labyrinth proved even more complex. The keys as a whole have been designated "an area of critical concern" under Florida's land use planning law, and Monroe County was in the process of preparing a growth management plan. If the state deems the local jurisdiction's plan unacceptable, the state may prepare the plan. Further, the Florida Audubon Society had initiated a major lawsuit over the provision of water and electricity to these undeveloped lands. And a number of state and federal agencies had an interest in the future of the area.

From a broader perspective, North Key Largo is an exaggerated example of what faces this nation--the increasing diversity of sharply focused public and private interests with a voice in the planning and regulation of significant land resources.

The situation in Key Largo posed several difficult questions. How could all of these interests be reconciled? How could the local, state, and federal processes ever be completed? (Certainly not by using the serial approach to permit processing that has characterized the traditional system of land use governance.) What ensures that a reconciliation once reached would be honored?

Providing a Forum

The first element of the Key Largo HCP process was defining a forum to convene the public and private interests involved. Based upon a request to convene the necessary local, state, and federal interests, Florida Governor Robert Graham issued an executive order establishing the North Key Largo Study Committee.

Participants' membership on the committee was by "self-selection"; that is, anyone interested could participate. While at first blush that method might appear to invite chaos, experience has proven the contrary. Over 120 people attended the first several meetings--interested laymen,

NORTH KEY LARGO
HABITAT CONSERVATION PLAN
AND SCOPING PROCESS

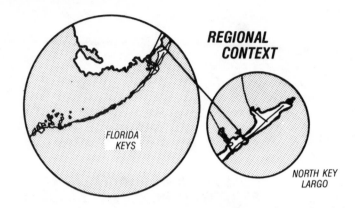

REGIONAL CONTEXT

FLORIDA KEYS

NORTH KEY LARGO

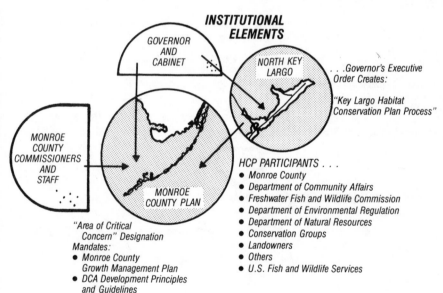

INSTITUTIONAL ELEMENTS

GOVERNOR AND CABINET

NORTH KEY LARGO

. . .Governor's Executive Order Creates:

"Key Largo Habitat Conservation Plan Process"

MONROE COUNTY COMMISSIONERS AND STAFF

MONROE COUNTY PLAN

"Area of Critical Concern" Designation Mandates:
- Monroe County Growth Management Plan
- DCA Development Principles and Guidelines

HCP PARTICIPANTS . . .
- Monroe County
- Department of Community Affairs
- Freshwater Fish and Wildlife Commission
- Department of Environmental Regulation
- Department of Natural Resources
- Conservation Groups
- Landowners
- Others
- U.S. Fish and Wildlife Services

HCP OBJECTIVES . . .
- Reconcile Wildlife and Development Concerns
- Conserve and Protect the Continued Existence of Endangered Species
- Be Consistent with and Augment Monroe County Growth Management Plan Objectives
- Provide Detailed Implementation and Funding for Habitat Conservation of North Key Largo . . .

31

BASIC ELEMENTS

- Habitat Protection Plan
- Long-Term Resource Management/Design Guidelines and Agreements
- Implementing Actions/Regulations
- Environmental Impact Statement Permits and Approvals

HCP
FOR
KEY LARGO

HCP SCOPING AND IDENTIFICATION OF PRELIMINARY THEMES AND VARIATIONS

. . . INTENT AND EVALUATION CRITERIA

- **Intent**
  To Explore a Range of Potential "Futures" for North Key Largo Pursuant to N.E.P.A. and to Optimize Land Uses for the Growth Management Plan and Endangered Species Protection Objectives.
- **Evaluation Criteria**
  - Ability to Enhance the Propagation and Survival of Endangered Species and to Comply with Endangered Species Act (16 USC, Sec. 1539)
  - Consistency with Growth Management Plan Objectives
  - Other Environmental Regulatory Requirements
  - Landowner Expectations
  - Feasibility: "Capable of Being Successfully Accomplished Within a Reasonable Period of Time Taking into Account Environmental, Technical, Economic, and Social Factors."

THEME 1: MAXIMUM HABITAT PRESERVATION

Variation A: Low-Density Development Under Status Quo Ownerships

Variation B: Cluster Development and for Density Transfers on or off Site

Variation C: Acquisition by Government or Conservation Groups

ISSUES AND CONSIDERATIONS . . .

- Landowner and Agencies' Objectives
- Long-Term Endangered Species Protection and Habitat Management Feasibility
- Transfer of Density Rights and Impact on Receiver Areas
- Market Demand

32

THEME 2: OPTIMIZE HABITAT VALUES UNDER MODERATE DEVELOPMENT
(3,000–6,000 D.O.s)
(_____ to _____ Acres of Development)

Variation A: Dispersed Development
Under Existing Conversions

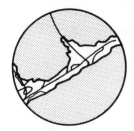

Variation B: Maximum Use of
Disturbed Areas

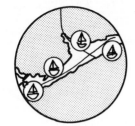

Variation C: Maximize High Value
Water-Oriented Development
in Minimal Acreage

ISSUES AND CONSIDERATIONS
- Endangered Species Protection
- Habitat Manipulation, Enhancement, and Management
- Disturbed Habitat Recovery Potential
- Height Restrictions
- GMP Objectives and TDRs
- Land Exchanges and Pooling Arrangements
- Landowner Expectations

THEME 3: MAJOR DEVELOPMENT
(6,000–13,000 + D.O.s)
(_____ to _____ Acres of Development

ISSUES AND CONSIDERATIONS
- Endangered Species Protection and
  Habitat Management—Especially Buffers
- Loss of Habitat
- GMP and Other Agencies' Planning Objectives

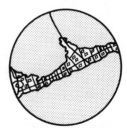

Variation A: Dispersed Development = Status Quo

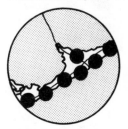

Variation B: High-Density
Cluster Development

TIMELINE . . .

GROWTH MANAGEMENT PLAN

Approved Growth Management
Plan Completed . . . Begin Implementation . . .

11/84 Growth Management
Plan Scenarios . . .

4/85

HABITAT CONSERVATION PLAN AND EIS

. . . Schedule Public Hearing . . .

End of Scoping

. . . Narrow Alternatives . . .

12/84 Begin HCP and   . . . Identify Significant
EIS Scoping . . .   Effects, Issues, and Concerns

4/85

(cont'd) ▷

ALTERNATIVES ANALYSIS
RESEARCH AND EVALUATION

. . . FIELD STUDIES (BIOLOGY)

To Determine:
- More Precise Under-
  standing of Characteristics
  and Requirements of Key Largo
  Ecosystem

. . . REVIEW PROCESSES

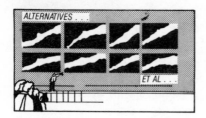

ALTERNATIVES . . .

ET AL . . .

. . . NARROWING OF ALTERNATIVES

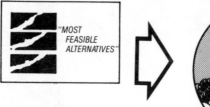

"MOST
FEASIBLE
ALTERNATIVES"

. . . SELECTION OF
PREFERRED ALTERNATIVE

Select Preferred Alternative . . .	. . . Prepare Response to Comments; Final EIS/HCP	11/15/85	Issue Final E.I.S./HCP . . .	. . . End of Process
6/1/85 . . . Prepare Draft EIS/HCP . . .	8/1/85 Circulate Documents for Public Review and Comment . . .		Finalize Project Agreement . . .	

PROPOSED HCP COMPONENTS

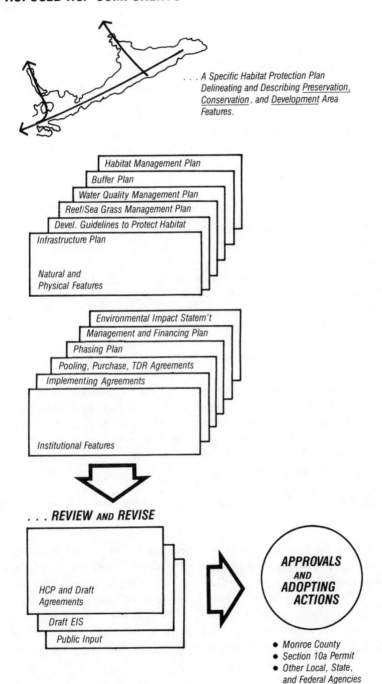

. . . A Specific Habitat Protection Plan
Delineating and Describing Preservation,
Conservation, and Development Area
Features.

Habitat Management Plan
Buffer Plan
Water Quality Management Plan
Reef/Sea Grass Management Plan
Devel. Guidelines to Protect Habitat
Infrastructure Plan

Natural and
Physical Features

Environmental Impact Statem't
Management and Financing Plan
Phasing Plan
Pooling, Purchase, TDR Agreements
Implementing Agreements

Institutional Features

. . . REVIEW AND REVISE

HCP and Draft
Agreements

Draft EIS

Public Input

APPROVALS
AND
ADOPTING
ACTIONS

- Monroe County
- Section 10a Permit
- Other Local, State,
  and Federal Agencies

high-level representatives of the various involved agencies, and deeply committed members of the public and private interests. As the meetings progressed, attendance leveled off to a more manageable number and rhetoric gave way to more thoughtful statements. In addition, a steering committee of 15 to 20 representatives of the key interests on the study committee was established. This group, in large part, was the negotiating group for the plan, and the study committee increasingly became a reviewing body.

Light at the End of the Tunnel

A key element of the HCP process is providing "light at the end of the tunnel," that is, maintaining participants' anticipation that the effort will succeed so that they will be willing to invest the significant time and resources required. To provide this light, two things are required: first, an understanding of the objective (in this case, a plan coupled with an enforceable agreement), and second, encouragement to keep the parties at the table (in part, provided by the governor's encouragement and the participation of other key state and federal agencies and groups). Recently, the county has increasingly indicated that the HCP will be a key element of its growth management plan, and the U.S. Fish and Wildlife Service has indicated that it will be the basis for reconciling concerns about federally listed endangered species. In short, this ad hoc process has become the site of the action.

The first several processes have been relatively expensive and time consuming. In each case, a major amount of time has been devoted to establishing the ground rules and the procedures. As this model becomes more common, it is likely that the time and expense involved will decrease and the quality of the plan increase, resulting in its increasingly broad application.

The Objective: A Habitat Conservation Plan and Agreement

The objective of the Key Largo HCP process is the development of a habitat conservation plan and agreement. The major elements of the plan include the establishment and dedication of conservation areas and designation of development areas, long-term funding and management, and appropriate restrictions on development. The agreement provides assurances to all parties that the plan will be honored. For the developer, it provides assurances that development will not be further restricted in

36

an effort to conserve wildlife; for the public sector, it provides assurances that the projected development will provide ongoing funding for the maintenance of the conserved habitat.

The habitat conservation plan has no regulatory effect until it is adopted by the various agencies as part of their regulatory or planning schemes. If the county, as expected, includes it in its growth management plan and if the Florida Game and Freshwater Fish Commission and the U.S. Fish and Wildlife Service use the plan as the basis for issuing permits for the taking of endangered species in connection with the contemplated development, the developer must comply with the regulatory procedures of the particular agency.

As the institutions involved reach a more pluralistic system of land use governance, specific legal concepts are evolving as well. The HCP, for example, prohibits governmental agencies from entering into agreements with the private sector that would "contract away their police power," but recent cases indicate that the courts are increasingly willing to find that a governmental agency may provide assurances or commitments or enter into covenants that will, in effect, inhibit the future exercise of their powers.

HCP's Relationship to the Scoping Process under NEPA

Like the National Environmental Policy Act (NEPA) of 1969, the habitat conservation planning process promotes the early participation of all those involved in a project to develop the scope of issues to be addressed in an environmental impact statement. The HCP process simply moves back a step and involves the interests in the plan's initial formulation.

Further, similar to NEPA, the HCP process uses alternatives modeling, that is, a study of "theme and variations." Participants explore reasonable alternatives as well as their impacts. For North Key Largo, the themes and variations range from high-density development, density transfers, pooling of interests, cluster development to maximize profits and minimize disturbance of the habitat, to no development. Any of these alternatives could include private action, such as pooling arrangements, and the provision of public funding.

This approach has a number of benefits. First, broad baseline studies can be avoided in favor of the focused studies necessary to decide between various alternatives. Second, the exploration of alternatives tends to promote cooperation and to lessen passionate rhetoric. The group does its best to fully and accurately explore agreed-upon themes and variations. Third, and perhaps most important, this process promotes the exploration of nuances that sometimes go unexplored when planning is undertaken in a politically charged and contentious atmosphere.

Thus, the group acting together can contemplate solutions that would normally be considered impractical or unattainable. The group, once assembled and working cooperatively, has enormous power. In Key Largo, for example, shortly after the process began, funding was needed to pay for staff work. If the landowners paid, it might taint the process, and in any case it would be difficult to get all 53 landowners to pay their share. The group's answer was to request Congress for an additional supplemental appropriation for the U.S. Fish and Wildlife Service, even though the 1984 federal budget bill had left committee and was being considered by the full Senate. Normally, at that point, the Senate will not entertain amendments for less than $100 million. Because of the number of interests making the request, however--developers, conservationists, and the governor's office--the amendment providing $100,000 to fund staff work was adopted.

Refining the Alternatives

A logical byproduct of self-selection is that the group acts by consensus. As issues are raised within the group, research is undertaken, solutions sought, and the alternatives slowly narrowed. While it is not absolutely necessary to reach a consensus on a preferred alternative--a decision can be left to the formal decision makers--it is likely that the committee will seek a preferred alternative. Not everyone must agree on a preferred alternative, but everyone should be able to agree that the plan fully and accurately describes the views of the participants with respect to the themes and variations addressed.

The Final Plan and Agreement

The final steps are preparation of the draft plan, the agreement, and the environmental impact statement.

The agreement goes beyond the plan; it provides assurances to landowners that development will not be constrained by further environmental problems and that funding commitments, remedies, and provision for unforeseen and changing circumstances and amendments have been included. The agreement must address the concerns of the courts with respect to commitments by governmental agencies to restrict the future exercise of their powers. The principles of equity are particularly important in this regard.

Following public review of the environmental impact statement and all of the concurrent agency processes, the plan is adopted and incorporated into planning and regulatory schemes, permits issued, and the agreement concluded.

Elements of the HCP Process

While the specifics of the Key Largo HCP process may be of interest to attorneys and to the land development community, the real value of the process is its implications for the way in which this nation addresses complex and sensitive land use issues—urban revitalization, water supply, air and water quality, the development of resources, and transportation. The HCP process anticipates and explores key elements of consensus planning. It includes several key elements:

o   the ad hoc nature of the institutional structure, which is outside any specific agency structure and situated between agencies as a cooperative undertaking;

o   the encouragement of trust among participants and the dispassionate exploration of various alternatives;

o   the self-selection of the participants, so that anybody who wishes to participate may do so, and the formation of a smaller steering committee, which enjoys the confidence of the larger group;

o   the analysis of alternative approaches, based on the example in NEPA, which contrasts starkly to the traditional approach of the private sector that increases the opportunities for confrontation;

o   the "reconciliatory" nature of the process, as opposed to compromise, making it a process by which a group can maximize individual interests; and o   the provision of certain assurances through a binding agreement, which ensures that the provisions of the plan will be honored.

Thus, the focal point planning approach can help resolve complex issues of land use planning and resource management to reconcile the interests of landowners, developers, governmental agencies, and public interest groups to the benefit of all.

Chapter 5

A PUBLIC OFFICIAL'S EXPERIENCE WITH PUBLIC/ PRIVATE DEVELOPMENT: BATTERY PARK CITY, NEW YORK
Barry Light

Battery Park City is a 92-acre piece of landfill in lower Manhattan opposite the World Trade Center. Then-Governor Nelson Rockefeller initiated the Battery Park City Authority in 1968 as a state authority with the "planning objective of revitalizing downtown and removing rotting piers." The unspoken objective was to dispose of 15 acres of landfill excavated during construction of the World Trade Center.

Soon after formation of the authority, the cordial relationship between Governor Rockefeller and New York Mayor John Lindsay soured. Because the project was on city-owned land, a lease had to be signed between the state and the city. The two public entities negotiated at arm's length, and the city's general inclination was to fight the state whenever possible. Consequently, the lease that was negotiated ensured an unbuildable and unmortgageable project.

In 1972, the Authority sold $200 million worth of general obligation bonds, hired a staff of 60 people, and set out to develop the property. But the combination of the problems with the lease, questions about the approach to negotiating, and New York's financial problems in 1975 ensured that nothing happened until the end of the decade.

With resolution of the city's and the state's financial problems in 1978-79, Governor Carey asked a team of people to work out Battery Park City's problems. The team had a better working relationship with the mayor and the governor, and it faced several fundamental questions: Should the site be turned into a park? Should it be abandoned? What should be done with it?

Barry Light is general manager of the Newport City Development Company in Queens, New York, and was president and chief executive officer of Battery Park City Authority.

The team's primary concern was how to meet the Authority's financial obligations. The $200 million worth of bonds were due in 1980, and, while interest on the bonds could have been paid out of bond obligations, principal could not. Someone had to raise the money or default would spread--from the Authority to the city to the state.

The team considered a variety of alternatives, including raising money from the state to pay off the bonds over a short period of time or undertaking a series of development options to pay off the money over a long period of time. It hired a major real estate consultant and two independent appraisers to appraise the property. Finally, the team performed a market analysis.

The Development Approach

The eventual program that was developed includes 6 million square feet of office space and 14,000 housing units, which will accommodate an estimated 30,000 workers and 55,000 residents. The Authority approached the problem by looking at it as though it were taking over a real estate investment trust that had failed. After a financial analysis, the Authority requested $8 million over four years from the New York state legislature. The Authority would build one office building and one housing project, in return for generating a certain amount of money. The Authority developed a business plan as though the project were being taken over by a private developer and, using a request for proposal (RFP), asked for bids to develop the property.

The most important point to remember when issuing an RFP is to know the goals for the project. The easiest to define is the monetary goal, but the public sector must determine the costs of construction, factoring in local labor, local construction, subsurface conditions, and so on. The public sector has to consider the financial parameters, in essence building a building on paper. At the same time, the bids must reflect a reasonable, realistic project. For Battery Park City, the proposals submitted were judged by two tests--income and quality. While the Authority was looking for the high bidder, it also had to ask whether the deal was realistic.

Other public goals--architectural design, affirmative action, art in public places, and security on the Authority's investment--were very hard to describe to private developers. Consequently, the Authority specified the rules up front to avoid any misinterpretation.

Before any developers submitted bids, the Authority developed a 150-page design guideline that specified siting, shape, height, and materials. The guidelines stipulated that on residential projects no architectural metal, architectural concrete, or exposed spandrell could be used and specified stone on the first two floors, setbacks, runner courses, head houses, roof materials, and window glazing. The guidelines contained some miscellaneous provisions--a time limit for architectural review of the proposals, the establishment of an art program using money collected in lieu of sales tax for public art, and designation of a park maintenance charge to the developer. Developers were not required to include a design in the bid, and the Authority had the right to veto the choice of architect.

To cover costs, the Authority charged a fee for submission of a proposal. Using those fees, the Authority hired a law firm to prepare certain documents. Leases for the commercial center, for example, ran to about 6,000 pages.

The Authority received 12 proposals for development of the commercial center.

Understanding the Opposition

Upon entering negotiations, the Authority assessed the relative strength of its opposition--and its opposition consisted of 12 large developers with a high degree of political strength. The Authority therefore had to be careful in its negotiations and had to make sure the basics of the deal were realistic. It had to understand the developers' concerns. For example, with a $10 million housing project financed by a Citibank or a Bank of America, the public sector will not be able to change the loan requirements. Developers are not going to change their financing strategy.

One of the Authority's initial tasks was to research the developers' backgrounds. Few development companies are publicly held, and few make public financial statements available. Most of the developers who submitted bids for Battery Park City would not make financial statements public. Thus, the Authority visited projects completed earlier by all of the developers who submitted bids and examined the firms' finances and backgrounds by checking with other public entities that had dealt with the developers.

Equal information about its opposition places the public sector on an equal footing with a developer. Negotiations become more honest and developers become more accurate. Knowledge gives the public sector strength in negotiations and the ability to sell the deal to constituents. It is critical to developing trust and effective partnerships between the public and private sectors.

A developer entering negotiations must understand the rules in a public/private negotiated development. Public/private negotiations require a knowledge of government regulations and an understanding of legal and political constraints. The developer must understand the public sector's concerns. The deal will be subject to public scrutiny and to the complaints of those who did not win and those who opposed the project.

The Development Agreement

After analyzing the bids and meeting with developers, the Authority selected Olympia and York, a Canadian developer, to develop the Battery Park City project. The two parties entered negotiations for the development agreement with different interests in minds--the Authority to carry out its financial mandate to make money for the state and to protect the bondholders and the taxpayers, and the developer to make a profit. As a landlord, the Authority had to work closely with the developer, even though the relationship was adversarial. The close working relationship did not happen overnight.

The parties had to negotiate terms of the land lease. While agreeing on the dollar amount of the land lease was easy, protections like security on the money were difficult. The developer wanted to offer participation in profits. The Authority wanted guaranteed rent.

The developer and the Authority settled on using a letter of credit. The developer would provide a letter of credit guaranteeing the amount of rent through completion of the project, and then, if it defaulted, the Authority would take the buildings. If the developer did not default, the letter of credit would be returned. When the Authority had letters of credit on file for the required $100 million guarantee, it realized that letters of credit are very risky. Court opinions have held that a letter of credit is not the same as cash, and the issue in this case was whether a letter of credit on a Canadian bank could be cashed by a public authority in the state of New York if the Canadian developer defaulted.

The Authority therefore wanted the developer to have a local bank, but all of the developer's banking instruments were in Canada. Because the relationship between the Authority and the developer had evolved into a good one, the parties were able to resolve the issue.

This personal relationship worked both ways. In the process of obtaining financing, Olympia and York's lender asked for some protection in case of default, and the Authority was able to discuss the problem with the lender and the developer.

Throughout the negotiations, the Authority's objectives for an affirmative action program, funds to subsidize a minority business enterprise, and relationships with labor unions raised the most difficult points. It took a year to resolve those issues.

The project had to be kept moving because at that period office space was in demand and financing was available. Soon thereafter, however, the economic situation deteriorated, and interest rates climbed to 18 percent. The public sector had to be willing to cooperate fully when the deal was to close, and it had to operate as though it were a

Architect's model of Battery Park City fully developed.

Rector Place as viewed from the Hudson River--architect's model.

Architect's rendering of the residential development in Battery Park City.

private company. Ultimately, timing was the key to success. The development opportunity happened to be right at the time.

The public negotiators had to learn to negotiate. Although people in government are able technicians and administrators, not many have the skill or experience required in negotiations--to be nice on Monday, an antagonist on Tuesday, and friendly again on Thursday. The public side had to learn when to come back to the table. And it had to act as a private developer. Despite the attitude that a government authority does not have to make money, the Battery Park City Authority had an obligation to pay off its bondholders, and the public authority had to develop the sophistication to act as a developer.

Conclusion

Was Battery Park City successful? In the sense that the project is underway, it has been successful. Some real problems remain, however. The negotiations were lengthy--2½ years for the housing project and two years for the office leases. Although a large developer like Olympia and York can wait six months and can carry $200 million or $300 million worth of financing, a small or minority developer cannot (thus excluding such developers from this process). Although equitable relationships were established for subcontractors, the kind of participation for small and minority firms the Authority desired did not occur.

Public negotiators should know what they are asking for, put it in writing, and then stick to it. Developers must be aware of all the public entity's goals and requirements. The developer's burden is to understand the public official's restrictions, particularly the political concerns. Once the deal is completed, the public sector becomes the developer's ally, for it is the public official's job, once negotiations are completed, to get the project done.

Negotiated public/private developments are complicated. If both sides deal with issues as problems to be solved, not irrevocable differences, a deal is possible. The Authority was fortunate in being outside the civil service rules that hobble many public officials, but it still is a public agency, negotiating a public deal, open to public scrutiny, and held politically accountable.

Chapter 6

STAKEHOLDERS ANALYSIS APPLIED TO THE REPUBLIC SQUARE DISTRICT, AUSTIN, TEXAS
Michael P. Buckley

Development, especially major development, affects more than the legally involved individuals and groups. These other interests, the "stakeholders," must be at least minimally satisfied with the proposed development, or they will oppose and possibly kill it. The term "stakeholder" implies more than "partner" or "party," which is limited to the legal participants in the project--the developer, the local jurisdiction, the lender. Stakeholders, in contrast, can also include affected individuals.

The first step in a stakeholders analysis is to identify the stakeholders, and the first step in identifying stakeholders is to determine the real development problem. If no real development problem exists, a public/private partnership is not necessary; the private sector would have pursued the development independently. In determining the problem, the parties must focus upon the minimum solution, setting the stage for the ensuing effort to reach a settlement on broader issues. And it helps to establish accurate costs early. Each participant in the negotiations must have a clear and realistic idea of the necessary financial commitments to see the project through to completion.

After identification of the stakeholders, five steps follow:

1. Explore each negotiator's viewpoint in advance. Query anyone with a stake in the effort--developer, city, local business leaders, community groups, unions--about their concerns and desires.

2. Determine the participants' relative authority. Who speaks for which segment during negotiations? Who is a reliable source? Who has influence on the decision makers?

Michael P. Buckley is president of Halcyon Ltd., a real estate development consulting firm.

3. List the city's broader interests. What does the city really need? Are its wants and needs greater than the project under negotiation can fulfill? Is the project a political plum for an elected official? Will it carry a broader agenda for community groups?

4. Agree on the major tasks to be completed and who is to perform them.

5. Use an explicit process for negotiating.

    o   Separate the problem from the people. Disengage the chief players--developer, city officials, local businessmen, community groups--from the issues being discussed. Make sure sessions focus on the real estate development product as a solution for problems.

    o   Focus on common interests and financial facts, not on personal positions. Seek common ground and build creatively on that foundation. Search for additional points of agreement within the boundaries of agreed financial and physical objectives.

    o   Search for options and alternatives with mutual gain. Make sure one segment does not benefit unfairly over another. Maintain an equitable approach to each stakeholder.

    o   Use objective value-oriented and financial criteria. Establish in advance that there will be no surprises for any of the participants concerning project cost, schedule, participation, input into the project, or any other conditions agreed upon during negotiations.

Developing a climate for effective public/private negotiation is often impeded by each party's stereotypes and fixation with its own problems and objectives rather than with understanding those of other stakeholders. Developers and public officials often encounter problems in negotiations because of their contrasting stereotypes and objectives (see Figure 1). Success, however, usually occurs by mutual resolution of problems, not by one stakeholder winning.

Austin's Republic Square District

The Republic Square District in Austin, Texas, developed by the Watson-Casey Companies, provides a useful illustration of a stakeholders

analysis. The project's goal was to redevelop Austin's underuse
warehouse district. A consulting team was charged with considering th
full scope of development--major commercial projects, infrastructure
public spaces, and supporting uses. Along with a program to achieve th
highest and best development of the district, the team was charged wit
identifying steps for implementing the project and the financing strateg
necessary to produce a fair return for the investment.

In Austin's Republic Square District, the development program had t
be derived from the needs of the stakeholders--those who are influence
by or can influence the success of the development--as well as from
realistic assessment of the developer's capacity and resources and th
project's potential success in the market. Thus, a development progra
can be designed to maximize the developer's return while responding t
the developing and shifting pressures of the market. It can als
influence neighborhood groups, city agencies, and other stakeholder
whose involvement can significantly facilitate (or significantly impair
the implementation of the program.

When properly conceived, large-scale public/private developmen
partnerships are a feasible and powerful tool to combat an area's declin
and underuse. Indeed, the record shows that such a partnership ca
revitalize an area like Austin's warehouse district that is in the mids
of accelerated deterioration or grossly underused. The ability to mak
the most of an area's potential, however, ultimately requires interactio
among numerous stakeholders, a comprehensive scope, and each sector'
participation in the risks and the rewards.

The stakeholders analysis performed for the Republic Square Distric
identified the critical issues and elements of the development progra
that satisfied the interests of the various stakeholders. It als
proposed approaches to the stakeholders' interests that influenced th
outcome of the eventual development.

Figure 1
DEVELOPER AND PUBLIC CONCERNS IN NEGOTIATIONS

The Developer's Viewpoint	The City's Viewpoint
--How can we limit the city's actions and decision points?	--How can we stay involved in decisions to safeguard the city's development objectives?
--Can we establish well-defined responsibility and a single authority within the various city actors?	--How many teams, departments, and staffs will be involved?
--How can we influence the city's choice of bond counsel to ensure an aggressive bond issue?	--Can the city defend a conservative and publically acceptable bond proposal? How can we limit our advance financial commitments?
--Can we convince the city of the need for creative public/private financing?	--What questions does the city need answered before proceeding on a creative public/ private financing scheme? Are we financing an unreasonable portion of the developer's risks?
--Can we predict the city's response to the developer's initiatives?	--How will the developer respond to the changing political climate?
--Can we stall the city's projections for revenue or participation long enough to establish our own true costs and returns?	--How can we get the best return for this once-in-a-lifetime opportunity?
--How can we use the city's effectiveness in facilitating the approval process?	--What checkpoints and reviews do we need to guarantee delivery of the product we expect?

--How can the city be managed
during design and development?

--How can the city's best
interests be served during
design and development? What can
we learn from problems that
occurred on other projects?

--What responses should we make
to the city's request for
clarification of value-added issues?
Why should we reveal our true
return?

--Can we trust these numbers?
How can we ensure a reasonable
return in exchange for a better
product?

Methodology

The catalyst for a partnership is based on identifying mutual interests and then targeting possible projects that enjoy the support of interested, public/private investment coalitions. Each side then undertakes specific steps, within its sphere of influence, to advance the purposes of the partnership.

A stakeholders analysis can provide a useful framework for making initial judgments about a strategic program for development, its timing and priorities, and the possible opportunities for or impediments to implementation. For the Republic Square District, the following issues were addressed:

o   Who are the key stakeholders and what are their attitudes toward development in the study area and in contiguous neighborhoods? What particular aspect of the Republic Square District interests them, and what might their attitudes be toward future development?

o   How powerful are the likely proponents and opponents with respect to a particular development concept?

o   Which type of development projects and related public improvements could the market and the various public/private stakeholders support that will also satisfy the developer's expectations for return on investment?

o   For any given development program, where will the strongest opposition come from? Which groups will be the strongest supporters? Which groups will be neutral or indifferent? To what degree do the various stakeholders share the same appreciation of problems and opportunities?

o   How does the program relate to mechanisms already in process or being currently proposed or advocated by key actors? How could parts of the new strategy be linked to existing mechanisms or combined with other proposals to achieve a consensus?

o   Among the sets who might support or oppose the development, what are the coalitions and alliances that exist or that could easily be developed?

The purpose behind such questions is to try to understand, predict, and prepare for the behavior of key proponents or opponents during implementation. At this stage, it is necessary to examine potential development through the eyes of particular stakeholders. The following summary of stakeholders' opinions and resources relates to the Republic Square District study area.

The Key Players: Who Are They, What Do They Need, and What Can They Contribute?

The major stakeholders in the Republic Square District development were various government and educational institutions, the city, the private sector, and neighborhood organizations. Their distinguishing characteristics are attributable to their different functions within the study area and the city, their respective self-interests, their attitudes toward development, and the resources and power each could contribute. Figure 2 categorizes stakeholders with respect to their interests and expectations, the role they could play, and the resources they could contribute and identifies the direction and the potential power stakeholders could exert during predevelopment or development.

Institutions

The dominant institutions in the area--the state government, the University of Texas, and Austin Community College--share a concern for "visible" and "symbolic" improvements in the area, including safety and security, public improvements (both infrastructure and public/recreational facilities), office and retail/commercial space, and adequate housing for employees and students. Most institutional members emphasized that the area should not close at night and suggested the use of an anchor for cultural and entertainment events.

As a group, the institutions regard future high-density development with guarded optimism. Although they share the sense that some development should occur because the timing and the area are right, they are reluctant to indicate just how much density is acceptable, their ability to compromise their differences, and their willingness to begin to attack some of the area's problems.

Their caution is attributable in part to the frequently cited belief that because the city is seeking to develop the blocks around City Hall, the city will determine the timing and direction of development in the

Figure 2
STAKEHOLDERS IN AUSTIN'S REPUBLIC SQUARE DISTRICT

STAKEHOLDER	INTERESTS/EXPECTATIONS/NEEDS	RESOURCES TO CONTRIBUTE	POWER		WHO INFLUENCES THE STAKEHOLDER	WHOM THE STAKEHOLDER INFLUENCES
			ADOPTION	IMPLEMENTATION		
o State Government o University of Texas o Austin Community College	o Attractive environment o Security/safety o Institutional needs met o Housing o A 24-hour environment	o Influence o Joint ventures, possibly in teleconferencing facilities o Office or video production space o Housing mortgage finance programs	+	+	o Strong community groups o Private interest groups o City	o Member institutions o Strong community groups o Private interest groups
o City of Austin	o Diversified housing o Public improvements o Retail amenities o Designation as a "special district" o Cultural uses o Height, view corridors o Scale and density	o UDAGs o Influence and support o Condemnation/eminent domain o Land writedowns o Bonds o CDBGs o Land o Tax abatement o Zoning o Capital and operating budget o Designation as a special district o Special assessment anticipation notes o Tax increment financing o Marketing/promotion o Signage	N	N	o Institutions o Community groups o Private interest groups o Voters	o Institutions o Community groups o Private interest groups o Voters

Stakeholder	Interests	Resources			Support	Key Actors
o Private Developers	o Diversified housing o Demolition and site control o Retail/commercial center o Recreational facilities o Public improvements	o Equity/syndication o Track record/expertise o Links with financial community o "Vision"	0	+	o Uncertain	o Uncertain
o Minority Groups	o Housing development o Commercial development o Public improvements o Recreational space and community facilities o Involvement and direct participation in development initiatives o Employment training and job placement	o Strong links with the political community o In-kind services o Publicity/marketing o Small business	+	+	o Minority development and financial community	o Minority development and financial community o City Council and politicians
o Special Interest Groups	o "Appropriate" scale and density o Transportation/traffic o Effect on neighborhoods o View corridors o Open space	o No fiscal support	+	++	o Uncertain	o City departments o City Council o Mayor

Key

++ = very powerful
+ = powerful
0 = not powerful
N = key actor with ability to veto

Republic Square District. As one respondent observed, "When the city decides it's ready to move ahead, they are, in essence, deciding for the others. Because of their size, the area's developers are in the position of taking cues from the city, not vice versa." Other institutional actors echoed this perspective; they contended that the city's ability to control the pace of the City Hall development and related capital improvements (for example, First and Third Streets) puts it in a lead position.

Several institutional members cited the need for a hotel/conference facility but could not agree about its location. Some felt it should enjoy a prominent location on Congress or on one of the city's waterfront sites. Others felt that the facility should reinforce existing downtown strengths or be used to create a new major commercial/destination point in the Republic Square District. Austin Community College members indicated the need for a video production facility--both live and studio--in the area. Because of the growth of video in the Austin market and its increasing popularity as a course of study, ACC projects the need for about 20,000 square feet of shared video production facilities. It also sees a growing need for associated office and classroom space. (State revenue bonds are available to finance these needs.)

Along with the need for a major destination/focal point in the Republic Square District, the institutions indicated a need to improve dramatically the area's physical and "psychological" image. The public's perception is shrouded by fears for safety and security. Several institutional spokesmen expressed concerns about the need to turn around the area's "market image," an objective that could be accomplished with well-integrated residential, institutional, and quality open space.

Several institutions perceived a strong need for housing for employees and students, particularly professional personnel and graduate students. Massive demolition and new construction are regarded as a necessary stabilizing tactic for the area. The institutions also recognized the needs of the growing elderly population and empty nesters and cited the importance of encouraging home ownership or rental opportunities for lower- and middle-income families. Thus, a goal for the area should be to encourage the formation of a stable, residential workforce.

Each institution recognized that critical, prerequisite elements for redevelopment in the area are substantial public improvements and assistance in site assembly. The institutions believe that by assembling large tracts of land and preparing them with the necessary public improvements, large-scale development is possible and desirable.

Neither the state, the University of Texas, nor Austin Community College is in a position to play a key role in the formation and acceptance of a development concept for the Republic Square District. Each stakeholder regards the city and the Watson-Casey Companies as the key catalysts for the Republic Square District. Some institutions could, however, use their networks to assist in the marketing of the development plan to the public and private sectors.

The City

The city regards the Republic Square District as an underused economic development area. City officials cited the district's vacant land parcels, underused warehouses and manufacturing space, and river views as potential development strengths. City officials have adopted a "wait and see" attitude, pending final positions on their City Hall project. Their power lies in the ability to structure and influence the development plan and its implementation. But their ability and willingness to commit resources would potentially affect not only the formation of the development concept but also its feasibility.

Most city officials interviewed want housing and complementary commercial uses for the area. Retail development and cultural/ entertainment uses are strongly needed. City officials' principal concern is to provide jobs and derive tax revenues from an area that at present yields marginal economic and social benefits. They view the area as the natural extension of the central business district but are concerned about scale, density, view corridors, height, parking, and "street life." The common theme is that redevelopment in the district should stay within the grain and character of Austin, not go against it.

The various subunits of the city government, however, have not reached consensus. While they may agree generally about the desired ends--jobs, taxes, redevelopment--there is little consensus about the means and the priorities of an overall development strategy for the Republic Square District.

The Private Sector

The private sector's perspective of development potential for the Republic Square District is ambivalent, ranging from "it's hopeless" and "why bother" to cautious optimism, given certain actions by the city. Most private respondents indicated, for example, that if a substantial program were undertaken to clear the land and if public improvements were installed, development could occur. In the absence of an overall, coherent strategy supported by a city/community coalition, however, developers believe that the warehouse area on both sides of Congress is too volatile politically and too unstable economically. An officially adopted plan would provide what one developer called a "sense of confidence and predictability" for the area and would encourage greater private interest in it. "Otherwise," as one developer noted, "why bother ourselves down there when the suburban areas have fewer hassles and cheaper land prices?"

Some private developers contend that with a substantial amount of site control, clustered, low-rise housing, related to an existing area of strength or stability, would be marketable and could create and capture the latent demand for close-in housing. Other developers cited the need to establish a large mixed-use project that would create sufficient momentum to generate demand in itself and reverse the area's negative image in a single step.

Neighborhood/Nonprofit Organizations

Many neighborhood organizations shared a similar perspective of the study area's needs--housing, new construction, and retail, recreational, and community facilities. Economic development in the form of jobs, developer-sponsored employment training, and job placement are also high priorities.

Several neighborhood organizations are extremely sensitive to the issues of participation in the Republic Square District's development plan and involvement in its implementation. Their power, collective or individual, would come during implementation; they have strong links to the City Council and several city agencies and could therefore thwart or enhance a given development tactic. Several groups are likely to rally around such issues as height, view corridors, public facilities, and traffic. They are typically aligned with the no-growth movement and could represent a potential obstacle to development.

The Potential for Coalition

At this point in the formation of a feasible development program for the Republic Square District, several statements can be made about the various stakeholders' motives, the potential for coalition, and the areas where a preliminary consensus can be achieved.

o   Begin demolition/land clearance and site control. All major stakeholders believe that an essential prerequisite for development is to remove blighted influences. Either the city or the developer should be the principal force in this effort.

o   Build on areas of strength and immediate market support, particularly on key sites. Most important, begin with a near-certain "winner" that has strong symbolic significance. The majority of the stakeholders, particularly the city and the private sector, contend that the boundaries of the Republic Square District should be regarded as a "special planning district." Initial development must begin with a project or projects that can serve as a rallying point for the area and its stakeholders; many respondents believe that symbolic value is as important as economic success.

o   Neighborhood-based organizations must receive more than a token response and participation. To prevent politically linked groups or potentially volatile issues from hindering prospective development, the developer should attempt to elicit the direct involvement of key neighborhood and minority groups and incorporate their interests into the development strategy. The various neighborhood groups have strong links to the minority political communities and should be regarded as an asset to work with.

o   A centralized city development and planning entity is necessary. At present, no one organization is responsible for uniting the fragmented public, institutional, and private entities into a rational and coherent framework. The city lacks the processes and the organizations to manage the forces of change and capture the available opportunities. A city-related entity is required to unite the area's resources and capabilities.

o   Physical development provides the opportunity for positive social, economic, and institutional change. The self-interests of the various public and private groups are inextricably tied to the potential for developing the area. Thus, the various redevelopment processes and products can effectively unite seemingly disparate entities while effecting positive social and economic change.

o   Take advantage of capable existing mechanisms and organizations. Several organizations in the area have been working in various aspects of the development or revitalization of Austin and its central business district. Any proposed development should capitalize on the inherent strengths of existing organizations.

o   Unite essential institutional and private organizations around specific project components. City officials recognize that implementing a given development strategy cannot be accomplished by any one organization or sector; the problems and opportunities reach well beyond organizational jurisdictions. All elements have to be engaged in improving the area and involved in the attendant costs, risks, and rewards.

Stakeholders analysis is a useful tool for formulating a development strategy for an area and for developing a basis of negotiation for the many actors that become involved in development. It is a technique that looks at the project from a communitywide perspective and determines potential allies and the position of opponents. The ultimate benefit of the process is the resolution of conflicts.

Note

[1] Roger Fisher and William Ury, Getting to Yes: Negotiating Agreement without Giving In (Boston: Houghton Mifflin Company, 1981).

SECTION 3

NEGOTIATION STRATEGIES

Understanding the opposition is a key element in formulating negotiating strategy. How to deal with the different actors is the subject of Section 3.

Private developers and the public sector alike must deal with the concerns of the neighborhoods surrounding a development project. Malcolm Rivkin, in "Negotiating with Neighborhoods," describes the settings and subjects for negotiations with neighborhoods or citizens. He includes three examples--White Flint Mall in Montgomery County, Maryland, the Hercules development in Wilmington, Delaware, and the Central Platte Valley development in Denver, Colorado.

John Delaney, in "Negotiating with Professional Staff," discusses the factors a developer and an attorney should consider when entering negotiations with the staff of a local government entity. The article includes an outline that serves as a checklist for negotiators.

In a different vein, Charles Siemon describes agency-to-agency confrontations in "Negotiating in an Intergovernmental Context." The paper notes that the missions and legal authorities of the agencies are key to basic negotiating tactics and stresses that preparation gives the negotiator the edge.

Chapter 7

NEGOTIATING WITH NEIGHBORHOODS
Malcolm D. Rivkin

Denver's Central Platte Valley includes some 1,700 acres of bottom land criss-crossed by railroad marshaling yards and punctuated by warehouses and small industries. Through the valley runs one of America's long-neglected "urban" rivers, best known for its capacity to flood adjoining property. Viaducts--many built generations ago--carry traffic above the valley, for people have little reason to go there. All in all, the valley is not a very appealing or desirable place--unless one considers that the Central Platte Valley happens to be next door to downtown Denver and is a stone's throw from some long-established neighborhoods. It is prime real estate.

The city sees the valley as its last major source of undeveloped land and wants it put to productive, tax-generating use. Large corporations hold major chunks of the valley and want to develop them. Neighborhood residents are concerned about the outcome, but they too, tantalized by the recent transformation of the river bank into bike paths and slivers of park, want something better than railroad tracks and weeds. The interests are many and divergent. For several months during 1984-85, however, they all came together under the aegis of the Platte Valley Development Committee, created by Mayor Frederico Pena to study, debate, and negotiate the future development of the tract.

The Platte Valley Development Committee is the most recent, and certainly the most complex, example of a phenomenon that has come to characterize how major urban development is accomplished in the United States--through negotiation. Long gone are the days when it was relatively simple for a developer to obtain zoning and build, merely in response to his own economic equation. While this approach still may

Malcolm Rivkin is president of Rivkin Associates, Bethesda, Maryland. He is an urban development planner specializing in complex development projects.

be common in sparsely settled suburban settings, certainly for new growth in built-up areas, developers have had to add the capability for negotiation to their tool kits. While the impetus to negotiate has come from the development industry, local governments themselves are now increasingly faced with the need to enter negotiations. Capacity to be an effective participant for the city has become an iron necessity.

Types of Negotiation

Negotiation occurs in four basic types of circumstances, three of which include neighborhoods or "citizens."

Developers and Citizens

The "traditional" setting for negotiation with neighborhoods involves a developer of a potentially controversial project who sets out to woo nearby residents of the site or other powerful citizen interests. The developer's objective is to strike a deal with citizens who could block a project when it comes up for zoning or other regulatory approval. The developer makes concessions to the citizens and appears before the regulatory body with their support.

Local Government and Citizens

In this case, the jurisdiction itself--seeking to locate a public facility like a waste transfer station or to encourage a private commercial project--enters into dialogue with affected citizens to obtain their support.

Local Government and Developers

Jurisdictions' negotiating directly with developers is now a frequent occurrence. Its purpose is more to work out cost-sharing arrangements for major infrastructure and amenities than to avoid controversy.

Multilateral Negotiations

For multilateral negotiations involving government, developers, and private citizens--like those for Platte Valley or the recently completed Copley Square project in Boston--the impetus is to resolve conflicts as well as to establish public/private cost-sharing arrangements.

Roots of Negotiation

Negotiation between the public and private sectors has been taking place in earnest for about a decade. It has multiple origins.

Important roots of negotiation are found in the environmental movement and heightened citizen activism of the early 1970s. Before the National Environmental Protection Act of 1969 (NEPA), people were much more likely to accept what developers did with their land. As rapid growth occurred, however, groups and neighborhoods challenged traffic congestion, pollution, and large-scale intrusion arising from development. As citizens' participation in local government became the order of the day in the 1970s, citizens began to "take back" the authority they had delegated to zoning boards and local councils and became very effective at stopping major projects. Somewhere along the line, more skilled developers recognized the possibility for compromise as a relatively inexpensive price for project approval. Some citizens' groups and neighborhoods, for their part, grew weary of constant battles and began to see they could force modifications and amenities that were in their interest, leading to the negotiations between developers and citizens that have marked some of the most successful examples of the technique.

Meanwhile, regulatory systems began to undergo modification. The old, rigid Euclidean zoning was modified in many communities by new techniques, such as planned unit development (PUD), incentive zoning, and the so-called developer-proffer system used in Fairfax County, Virginia. The new instruments provided opportunities for tradeoffs, compromises, bonuses, and a developer's contributions to mitigate adverse impacts. Thus, government began to sanction negotiation.

Creation of the Urban Development Action Grant (UDAG) program in the late 1970s was a major spur to negotiated development involving local government as well as citizens and developers. UDAG got cities into the business of making deals in a way they never had been before. Each UDAG project is different, with few established ground rules. Teams of city officials and their advisors sit down to bargain with developers and their advisors about how the federal and local funding will be used and what project elements and financial commitments the developers will effectuate in return.

UDAGs also carried with them a requirement for environmental assessment and the implicit threat that if interested parties (that is, the citizens) requested a full environmental impact statement, a project could be tied up for months or years. Thus, cities were forced to become sensitive to impacted neighborhoods and, in some cases, to negotiate with those neighborhoods for amenities and facilities clearly perceived as to their benefit.

The most recent force for negotiation has been the urban fiscal crisis of the 1980s. UDAGs aside, the drying up of federal funds for urban infrastructure has forced some cities to seek new ways to support needed public works. Private developers, for their part, especially in high-value urban sites, have needed public actions and public funding to make complex projects work. These requirements have led to new forms of public/private partnerships, ranging from pooling private and city funds, to cost-recovery approaches where initial public outlays are repaid from the developer's profits, to, more frequently, tax increment financing and special taxing districts--all cases where individual deals are struck as a result of specific project negotiations.

What Can Be Negotiated

The subjects amenable to negotiation now cover just about every physical and operational element in a development project. They go far beyond matters normally treated in a zoning review--even in the most flexible PUD situation. Examples include:

o   use and mixture of uses
o   densities
o   height, setback, and orientation of activities
o   landscaping and buffering
o   internal street systems and pedestrian pathways
o   exterior design and materials
o   lighting
o   methods of handling and retaining storm drainage, effluent discharge, and solid waste
o   compensation for impacts on services and land values in adjacent areas
o   income and socioeconomic characterization of residents
o   security
o   staging and timing of development.

Last, and by no means least, is the matter of how to share front-end costs between public agencies and the private developer for supporting infrastructure on extremely complex projects.

Cases

This section describes three examples of negotiation, concentrating on situations where citizens were involved as negotiating parties and the resolution of conflict was a principal objective.

White Flint Mall--Montgomery County, Maryland

White Flint is a 750,000-square-foot specialty shopping center featuring Bloomingdale's, Lord & Taylor, and I. Magnin. It is one of the most successful examples of developer/citizen negotiation. Opened in 1978, it was the only major commercial project built in Montgomery County, Maryland, during a prolonged sewer moratorium in the 1970s.

Like many other situations of its kind, negotiation for White Flint started because someone made a terrible mistake. Bloomingdale's picked a site for its department store whose location looked perfect and required only rezoning. It launched a massive sales campaign in the county but did not consult with the nearby neighborhood. It spent hundreds of thousands of dollars in front-end costs and promotion, but the rezoning effort failed. Citizens mounted effective opposition, and the application was denied.

Still wanting to enter the lucrative Washington market, Federated Stores, Bloomingdale's parent company, picked another site whose owner was interested in building a much larger shopping center. The site was an abandoned golf course, gone to seed with minibike trails, that also bordered a settled neighborhood and required rezoning. The proponents then hired a new attorney and a new planning advisor, and negotiations began.

This time, the project team went to the neighborhoods before a single line was drawn on paper and before the hint of rezoning leaked to the press. The project team and the citizens entered a year-long negotiation process. While few in the neighborhood were happy with the idea of a major shopping center, they were frightened at the alternative high-density residential and office uses that could be put on the property and did not want the site to remain a festering sore. These goals were the thread of mutual interest that held the often arduous negotiations together.

In return for neighborhood support, the proponents made major concessions on design and management of the facility and executed legally binding written agreements with the neighborhood association to guarantee performance. No one appeared in opposition at the hearing, and the zoning was readily approved.

The legally binding agreements involved commitments by the developers on several physical and operational features, including a deeply landscaped perimeter buffer zone. The agreements permitted the neighborhood to review detailed site plans, and they indemnified the property values of adjacent homeowners. It was this last measure, resolving citizens' fears of lowered property values, that became the major catalyst for support.

In actual fact, property values have soared since the center was built, and the developer has never had to make good on that commitment.

White Flint is one of the most successful shopping centers in the country. The neighborhoods like it, and it provides numerous jobs for their teen-aged children. When the builder strayed from his landscaping agreement during construction, the citizens, armed with the protocol, got the county to threaten denial of occupancy permits, and the builder soon complied. The citizens continue to monitor performance.

The Hercules Development--Wilmington, Delaware

Hercules is a successful example of city/citizen negotiation on a highly controversial project all parties wanted. It took place in the early 1980s and was inspired by a UDAG.

Hercules is Wilmington's second largest employer with a workforce of over 1,000. Its downtown office headquarters were outmoded, and the company announced its intention to leave for a suburban site. After the initial announcement triggered public protest, Hercules agreed to stay, on three conditions:

o   that the city would locate a suitable site and make it available quickly

o   that the city would arrange financing at sufficiently favorable
     terms so that development costs to Hercules would be no more than on
     a suburban site

o   that construction could begin quickly.

The city located a large parking lot at the edge of downtown as a
site and applied for a UDAG of $16,878,000, intending to loan the UDAG
funds to Hercules at a nominal rate to supplement its own resources.

The problem triggering negotiation was the residential land use
abutting and near the site. Three neighborhoods were affected whose
residents ranged from young middle-class couples to poor blacks to
elderly people on fixed incomes. Under the terms of the UDAG
application, the applicant must demonstrate citizens' participation in
the process. More important, any interested party could request an
environmental impact statement before the grant is awarded. In that
case, the process would take many months, and Hercules unequivocally
stated it would walk away if such a delay ensued.

The city had never faced such a situation and resolved to try to
negotiate some form of mutual agreement with the neighborhoods before it
submitted the formal application. It then retained a planning advisor to
guide the negotiation process over a two-month period.

The Negotiation Process. The neighborhoods and their residents held
quite disparate views and had many grievances with the city.
Nevertheless, they also did not want Hercules to leave town. Like the
White Flint case, they did not want to retain the current use (the
parking lot) and were afraid of other potential uses for the site. These
were the threads of common interest that kept both sides talking during
negotiations.

A joint neighborhood committee was established to represent the
citizens. Respected political figures lent credibility to the process,
and city officials became confident enough to enter negotiations
directly. The planning advisors were able to win the confidence of all
parties and to formulate proposals that addressed the citizens' concerns.

Other technical consultants to the city were made available to test
the proposals for feasibility, and Hercules agreed to abide by the
agreements reached.

71

The Outcome. After several weeks of discussion, a formal protocol was drafted summarizing the major requests by the citizens to which the city was ready to agree. It also contained a commitment by the neighborhoods to support the project. The draft protocol was reviewed and revised in a final flurry of marathon negotiations before the UDAG hearing deadline. It was signed by the mayor and the neighborhoods' designated leaders and endorsed by the city council. Among the matters covered were the following commitments by the city and Hercules:

o   design controls on the building and on treatment of parking and the site;

o   controls on noise emissions during construction;

o   traffic controls to prevent use of neighborhood streets by vehicles destined for the central business district, including institution and enforcement of resident parking permits;

o   institution of zoning controls to prevent conversion of residential property to nonresidential use;

o   a revised area physical plan directed toward neighborhood protection;

o   immediate improvement of certain neighborhood services (trash collection, storm drainage);

o   a five-year capital improvement program for the neighborhoods with certain high-priority public works;

o   efforts to preserve housing for present occupants, including priorities for public rehabilitation loans and grants, city representation to banks for additional loans, and a long-term strategy to retard displacement of renters and low-income property owners; and

o   earmarked funds from Hercules's loan repayment for a neighborhood development foundation whose activities would be supervised by the city. (The funds would range from $87,500 to more than $100,000 annually over a period of 20 years.)

The UDAG was approved, the project was built, and the city and Hercules kept the agreements.

The Central Platte Valley--Denver, Colorado

Although the Central Platte Valley project is still undergoing multilateral negotiation and there is little to report in the way of outcome, it is a useful case to highlight some aspects of negotiation.

In many respects, the impetus for developer-initiated negotiation in the Platte Valley was very similar to that for White Flint. Almost a decade ago, one of the principal railroad owners in the valley decided to phase out its trackage and develop the property. It hired a design team, which produced an extremely detailed physical plan. Because the site lacked good access, it was clear to the railroad that some cost sharing with the city or state for infrastructure was essential. Once the plan was presented, the city appointed a blue-ribbon committee of officials and civic leaders--mainly from the business community--to spend over a year in studying the proposal. The panel endorsed the project and its multimillion dollar public expenditure. In the course of this arduous and expensive process, however, no one bothered to consult the nearby neighborhoods. Citizens unleashed a storm of protest, and the project was stopped for almost a decade.

In reviving the idea of development in 1982, the railroad took as a partner a skilled local development group that had just negotiated a successful rezoning with citizens elsewhere in the city. The new developers commissioned extremely detailed traffic, utilities, soils, and environmental studies and only the rough outlines of a concept plan. When a local city councillor announced he would form a citizens' coalition for the valley from affected neighborhood groups, the developers actively encouraged its establishment. In 1983, over a period of several months, the developers and their team met regularly with the coalition, shared fully with the members the detailed technical studies, reviewed, listened, and debated the concept plan, which addressed many of the citizens' concerns, and were extremely frank on the economic factors surrounding the interest in the project. The citizens were not forced to endorse the project, but the climate of mutual respect and trust that was established prepared the way for the tough multilateral negotiations begun in 1984.

The Platte Valley Development Committee is as wild a mix of negotiating parties as the West can offer. Created by Mayor Pena, the committee is charged with arriving at both a plan and a cost-sharing formula for the valley. Chaired by a council member, the committee includes elected officials, three major developers, the citizens' coalition, and representatives of the business community. It has been meeting in marathon sessions and at rural retreats since the spring of 1984.

Just about every issue one can imagine is being discussed in the sessions--from the city's development objectives to cost sharing for highways, to traffic generation, urban design, and neighborhood impacts. Perhaps never before has such a multidimensional negotiation process existed, and it will require infinite patience by all parties to reach a mutually acceptable conclusion. The jury is still out on whether such diverse interests can be successfully accommodated.

Essentials for Negotiation

Each setting for negotiation has its own special aspects, but a successful negotiation process has seven fundamental requirements.

1. All parties have to want to negotiate and to stick with a process that often seems long and fruitless. Everyone must be a stakeholder, perceiving some important benefits if a project is designed and built and some sense of loss if it is not. For public agencies and developers, that requirement is pretty easy. When citizens get involved, however, it is not so simple, and many negotiations have broken off because community interests have felt it was just not worth the effort. It helps if citizens do not like the present use of the land or fear alternative uses--as has characterized each example in this chapter. So long as citizens believe they can get a better deal from the other side of the table than leaving the property in its present state, the impetus to continue to bargain remains.

2. Sensitivity to other viewpoints is necessary. Negotiation is no role for the thin-skinned on any side, and all parties have to be prepared to make some compromises.

3. Clear channels of communication during the process and a clear structure for the negotiation setting are required. Negotiations

are invariably "informal," but they have to include face-to-face discussions with people who can make decisions or (when representatives of interest groups are involved) can go back to their principals for ratification of points and conclusions.

4. Technical skill is needed. This factor is particularly critical because options have to be tested--for physical and economic feasibility--as decision making evolves. Sometimes the technicians (planners, lawyers, architects, engineers, and so on) are the negotiators. Sometimes they are there to back up the principals, but their technical skill must be available.

5. A written protocol or other documentation should be the concluding step in the process. It should spell out responsibilities of the parties for the items negotiated, and it should be legally enforceable. Without such documentation signed by the parties involved, it is difficult to control compliance once construction begins.

6. Some means of monitoring compliance during construction and operation of the agreed-upon project should be established during negotiations.

7. Financial resources must be available to sustain the negotiations. Negotiation is costly, involving commitment by private developers and public agencies to pay for the services of professionals over and above normal project planning costs. It puts a tremendous burden of time and expense on the citizens who are stakeholders. In Denver, the Platte Valley Development Committee is getting help from city staff, but it has also sought foundation funding to fuel the process. In one instance, a developer paid for professional assistance to a potentially hostile neighborhood group simply to establish some reasonable basis for negotiation. The financial compromises, often significant, have some effect on the project's profitability. Negotiation is no easy or "inexpensive" process.

Looking to the Future

Cities and developers need to consider a number of implications in their efforts to work together.

Many more cases of negotiated development will occur. So long as the urban fiscal crisis of the 1980s deepens, cities and developers both will need to sit across the table from each other to work out deals. As the sites for major development increasingly become leftover or bypassed land in the midst of settled areas, input from citizens' groups will be a potent factor in determining the scale and nature of final projects. Lead times for major development will become increasingly longer and more costly to accommodate negotiation. Regulatory codes and municipal budgeting will have to be readjusted to sanction and accommodate negotiated agreements. Finally, local jurisdictions will need to become entrepreneurs and add professionals with entrepreneurial ability to their staffs and rosters of consultants. It will no longer be possible to passively wait for new sources of development and ultimate revenue. Promotion of the city is only one part of the picture. City officials will have to take an active role in brokering deals among developers and their own constituents. For many cities it will be a new role, and it will make the control and direction of urban development more exciting.

Chapter 8

NEGOTIATING WITH PROFESSIONAL STAFF
John J. Delaney

While decisions affecting land use could once be predominantly considered the application of objective standards found in zoning codes and other public policies to development proposals, that is no longer the case. Subjective issues, such as aesthetic, cultural, and spiritual values, can now enter into land use decisions. The transition is nicely captured by comparing a 1905 to a 1954 judicial opinion.

In 1905, the New Jersey Court of Error and Appeal found that "[a]esthetic considerations are a matter of luxury and indulgence rather than of necessity, and it is necessity alone which justifies the exercise of the police power to take private property without compensation." [City of Passaic v. Paterson Bill Posting, Advertising and Sign Painting Company, 62 A. 267 (N.J. 1905)] In contrast, in 1954, the U.S. Supreme Court found that "[t]he concept of the public welfare is broad and inclusive. The values it represents are spiritual as well as physical, aesthetic as well as monetary. It is within the power of the legislature to determine that the community should be beautiful as well as healthy, spacious as well as clean, well-balanced as well as carefully patrolled." [Berman v. Parker, 75 S.Ct. 98, 102 (1954)]

These statements reflect the distance traveled by the courts in recognizing aesthetic, cultural, and spiritual values as a basis for regulating land use. The past decade has witnessed a breakthrough in these new values' upholding a variety of regulations, ranging from housing and lifestyle to historic preservation.

While Berman v. Parker was a case involving eminent domain, the paragraph quoted earlier has been cited in not less than 35 cases upholding restrictive police power or ordinances of local government. [See, for example, Village of Belle Terre v. Boraas, 94 S.Ct. 1536 (1974); Construction Industry Assn. of Sonoma County v. City of Petaluma, 522 F.2d 897 (9th Cir. 1975); and Penn Central Transportation Co. v. City of New York, 98 S.Ct. 2646 (1978).]

John Delaney is a partner in the law firm of Linowes and Blocher, Silver Spring, Maryland.

Today, many subjects of land use regulation involve the use of highly subjective criteria and standards. They include ordinances dealing with preservation of historic and architectural landmarks, conditional/contract zoning, site plan and site design review, optional method and overlay zones, planned unit and mixed-use developments, and floating zones. It is difficult for the framers of these ordinances to articulate objective standards to guide the public, the government agency, or the private parties seeking development approval. One person's "aesthetic" or "spiritual" value (a spacious community, for example) may be another person's nemesis (a lack of affordable housing in the community). Moreover, the opportunity for regulatory abuse is greater when dealing with subjective ordinances. Exactly what does "compatible" mean?

On the other hand, when ordinances become too detailed, they may severely restrict or entirely eliminate discretion for the agency and flexibility for the developer.

This conflict between the need for standards and the need for flexibility may be irreconcilable. The risks involved are simply part of the public/private negotiation process. But professional staff should use certain guidelines to approach negotiations, supplied here as a checklist.

I.   Perceptions.

Before negotiating, consider:

A.   What is the professional staff's perception of itself and its role?
     1.   Strong staff/weak staff?
     2.   Strong board/weak board?
     3.   Does the staff play an independent, professional advisory role in implementing board policy, or does it anticipate the likely board decision in each case and prepare its recommendations accordingly?
     4.   Does the staff "take a position" or merely "discuss issues," leaving the determination to the board?

B.   What is the public's perception of the staff?
     1.   See A1 through A4 above.

2.   Does the staff act consistently in most cases? In exercising professional judgment, is the staff affected by the "politics" of the case?

3.   Does the staff enjoy the confidence of:
     a.   The board?
     b.   The public?
     c.   The development community?

C.   What is the developer representative's perception of his role?
     1.   Narrow: solely to advance the client's interests in an adversarial forum?
     2.   Broad: to demonstrate that the client's interests coincide and mesh with the public interest?

II. Negotiation Strategies.

     Consider:

A.   Timing: When should the staff first be consulted? (The answer depends upon the nature of the project and the nature and character of the staff. In most instances, particularly when dealing with a strong staff, consultation with the staff should occur before or immediately after concept plans are prepared. Doing so enables the public sector to identify and ward off potential adverse effects early and can be cost effective for the developer by enabling him to identify problem areas and make the necessary decision either to modify or abandon the project.)

B.   Precedents: Does the staff tend to view concessions gained from other developers in prior projects as a "floor" for future negotiations? (If this tendency exists, the developer must be prepared to distinguish this project from the prior ones.)

C.   Attitudes: Does the staff view the zoning envelope as:
     1.   Merely an indicator of maximum bulk/density from which each project must expect to descend?
     2.   An accrued and vested right in the developer that must be accommodated in reviewing the project?
     3.   And what is the view of the courts on this question?

D.   What is the propensity of the board to follow the staff's recommendation?

E. Exactly what is to be negotiated? (Finite constraints imposed by the ordinance--setbacks, traffic impacts--are usually not negotiable unless specifically waived by the ordinance, but the rest of the development package--siting, landscaping, public amenities--and its external effects are subject to negotiation.)

F. What is the developer's "bottom line"?

G. When should the developer's "bottom line" be put on the table? (The answer depends on several factors, including the number of tiers in the review process, attractiveness of the project, development schedule, nature and extent of citizens' involvement, the developer's past record, the staff's credibility and ability to finalize an agreement, likelihood of an impasse, the public sector's priorities and goals. It is generally not advisable to put all the cards on the table at the outset, particularly for a multitiered, highly politicized review process or where the staff is weak in relation to the board.)

III. Implementing the Negotiated Agreement.

     Consider:

A. With whom is the agreement to be finally concluded?
    1. Staff?
    2. Board?
    3. Legislative body (mayor and council)?

B. Does a prohibition against conditional or contract zoning exist?
    1. Conditional and contract zoning are prohibited in some jurisdictions, based upon the premise that they violate the provision of "uniformity" in most zoning enabling acts, that the local legislative body is prohibited from bargaining away its police power, that they disrupt the basic comprehensive plan and subvert public policy, and that restrictions in a particular zoning district should not be left to private agreements between individual applicants and the municipality. See Baylis v. City of Baltimore, 148 A.2d 429 (Md. 1959).
    2. Other jurisdictions allow conditional/contract zoning, particularly where it is authorized in enabling acts. See Sylvania Electric Products, Inc. v. City of Newton, 183 N.E.2d 118 (Mass. 1962).

3. Even where conditional/contract zoning is frowned upon, problems can usually be avoided when the "conditions" are imposed by (or the contract executed with) government entities other than the local legislative body. See generally _State ex rel Zupancic_ v. _Schimenz,_ 174 N.W.2d 533 (Wis. 1970); _Town of Somerset_ v. _Montgomery County Council,_ 181 A.2d 671 (Md. 1962); _Scrutton_ v. _County of Sacramento,_ 79 Cal. Rptr. 872 (1969).

C. How is the agreement to be formalized?
   1. By developer accepting conditions imposed in:
      a. Formal report of staff or board?
      b. Approval resolution of local legislative body?
   2. By developer executing a formal agreement with public body (staff, board, legislative body)?

Chapter 9

NEGOTIATING IN AN INTERGOVERNMENTAL CONTEXT
Charles L. Siemon

Intergovernmental negotiations arise in two contexts: a developer who needs approval of more than one government agency and a public agency that requires approval of another government agency.

The first point to be made about intergovernmental negotiations is almost too simple to mention, but it is nevertheless very important and much abused. Know the mission of the agency entering negotiations. Agencies' missions are usually well defined in the statutes that created them and in the rules and regulations they implement. For example, negotiations are underway involving Monroe County, two agencies of the state of Florida (the Department of Environmental Regulation and the Department of Natural Resources), and the Army Corps of Engineers. These four agencies have four different missions, and by the fifth round of negotiations, they began to delineate and understand each agency's mission. They can now work toward a negotiated framework that makes some sense.

Understanding the other agencies' legal authority to act is also important. In innumerable instances, a representative of a local government or state agency has entered intense negotiations with another agency without fully understanding the other agency's legal authority. For example, the U.S. Post Office claims that local jurisdictions have no authority over the Post Office, but, in fact, the Post Office is exempt from local regulations only when no practical alternative exists. The U.S. Post Office can be made to conform to local regulations unless it can meet that very difficult burden of proof.

Charles Siemon is a partner in the law firm of Siemon, Larsen & Purdy, Chicago, Illinois.

In the same vein, one must know precisely one's own agency's authority--and be firm in that position. For example, in the New Jersey Pinelands, a crazy-quilt patchwork of legislation established a regional agency, but it was not clear how this regional agency related to other state agencies and their activities in the Pinelands. The Pinelands commission was convinced that it should take a very firm position from the beginning as to the commission's authority over other stage agencies. Written legal opinions can reinforce one's position of strength. The agency was able to bluff every other state agency, including the Department of Environmental Regulation and the Department of Transportation, because it had a written legal opinion that defined its role in developing the comprehensive regional plan.

High-level meetings speed up negotiations. Although high-level governmental officials are always busy, have many responsibilities, and are usually underbudgeted, including them in negotiations is worth it. Meetings of fourth-level functionaries elongate the process, because they have to return to their supervisors for answers.

It is easier to take control of the situation by having a short, well-written document in hand outlining the agency's goals and objectives, the critical points, and the agency's position. This element is critical. A piece of paper on the table gives the negotiator a leg up. Further, good preparation encourages participation by the agency head or the senior agency official.

In conclusion, two requirements ensure successful negotiations with another government agency--an understanding of the mission (and the ability to convince the opponent of that mission) and the ability to show how that mission fits with the opponent's mission and how mutual ground can be achieved. In defining missions and how they fit together, the negotiators can develop a framework for subsequent negotiation.

Casualness about intergovernmental negotiations is unlikely to contribute to good and amicable settlements. Delay is an enemy in any process involving a bureaucratic institution. If anything, preparation needs to be greater when one is dealing with another public agency. Usually no legal capacity is available to compel a decision. Absent some political influence, negotiating an agreement with another governmental agency is not subject to external constraints. The prospects of being able to go to court for relief are very small. Only a positive program will lead to successful negotiations.

SECTION 4

CONDITIONAL ZONING APPROVALS

A number of zoning techniques--planned unit developments, flexible (performance) zoning, and mixed-use zoning--provide for variations in standards and uses if they are compatible with characteristics of the site and the neighborhood. Approving these techniques usually requires extensive negotiations, culminating in approvals conditioned upon certain agreed-upon requirements that become in effect implied contracts.

Section 4 includes two articles that describe experiences in negotiating zoning approvals. John Griffin, in "The University Place Experiences" describes the negotiations that took place to obtain approval of a mixed-use project in Cambridge, Massachusetts.

In "Negotiating Conditional Zoning Approvals," Joseph Clancy describes classic examples of negotiation--Mount Prospect, Illinois, and Washingtonian Center, Montgomery County, Maryland. These examples illustrate how local, controversial issues that may or may not be directly relevant to the project overwhelm negotiations for rezoning.

Chapter 10

THE UNIVERSITY PLACE EXPERIENCE
John P. Griffin, Jr.

Although zoning is among the most localized of activities, the experience at University Place in Cambridge, Massachusetts, is applicable to other jurisdictions. The primary techniques used in the negotiation process were threats, tears, and, finally, outright capitulation.

University Place, a project of Hines Industrial, was built on land that had been used as a parking lot and was owned by Harvard University. Harvard decided, under pressure from the city of Cambridge, to develop the land for private, not university-related purposes, but only if the project were economically viable.

Harvard officials did not want to suffer the experiences of some previous developers in the area. Charles Square--a proposed, large mixed-use development, with hotel, offices, expensive condominiums, and a garage on an abutting parcel--had been under negotiation with the various organizations of Cambridge for approximately five years and had gotten nowhere. MIT, another Cambridge institution, had bought a piece of property in another section of Cambridge approximately 15 years earlier, and citizens held protest marches almost monthly against the proposed conversion of that parcel to business uses. Harvard did not want to buy into that pattern. It wanted a completed project that was financially viable. At the same time it did not want to antagonize the citizens.

Environment

The neighborhood is a microcosm, not only of Massachusetts, but perhaps of the world. The existing parking lot was ugly but necessary

John Griffin is a partner with Rackemann Sawyer & Brewesser, specializing in land use law.

because people like to park in Harvard Square, where parking is more of a privilege than a right. Adjoining the rear of one parcel is an order of cloistered Anglican monks, who never participated directly in the negotiations.

Next to the monastery is a very expensive cooperative that was built beyond what is the historic course of the Charles River. The residents' primary concerns were loss of free parking on land owned by Harvard and the possibility that the construction of the project would result in their building's sinking. The structure is on wooden piles on filled land that have to be kept wet to prevent their rotting. The residents of the cooperative had visions of University Place dropping the water level and putting them into the Charles River. Moreover, the sludge upon which the cooperative is located is historic--being garbage that was dumped in the Charles River in the 17th century--and residents wanted it undisturbed.

On the other side of the proposed project is the Charles Square project, and on the corner is an apartment building owned by Harvard. Inhabited by long-term Harvard students, it had been the subject of a rent withholding protest for approximately eight years.

Although residents of the area did not want the parcel to continue as a parking lot and wanted to see it developed, the question was how to develop it without getting caught up in the morass other developers have experienced.

Community Interests

Harvard University and Hines Industrial decided to go to the community first and find out what they wanted. The Cambridge/Harvard community is extremely well organized, including several neighborhood groups--Neighborhood 10, Neighborhood 7, the Harvard Square Businessmen's Association, the Harvard Square Defense Fund, and more. The discussions revealed that what the groups really wanted was a mixed-use development. They wanted the parcel to mark the dividing line between the businesses in Harvard Square and the residences in their neighborhood. So Hines and Harvard created an ad hoc committee comprised of the leaders of the various neighborhood groups, city officials, the planners, and members of the city council to work with the residents to propose a suitable design. The architect Harvard and Hines ultimately chose for the project had experience and showed sensitivity in designing buildings in controversial areas.

Hines formulated a conceptual design after performing massing and economic studies and deciding what would work on the site. Hine's proposed project was a reasonable design for that neighborhood: 200,000 square feet of first-class office space, a 500-car underground parking garage, and approximately 80,000 square feet of luxury condominiums built on air rights over the garage.

Hines kept all the neighborhood groups involved--politicians as well as neighbors--and then made sure that they dealt with more than just the leadership. They held a series of meetings to discuss the project, show the models, talk about problems, and refine the design as necessary, changing access here, putting a park there where buildings were originally planned. In so doing, Hines kept the neighborhood consensus together.

Hines produced letters of recommendation from cities where they had done business before attempting to do business in Cambridge. It was rather extraordinary to be able to get the planning directors or planning board chairmen of cities where they had built the first major development to attest that the developer had delivered on what it had promised. The legal basis for putting agreements in writing in Massachusetts is shaky at best, so the developer had to establish that it could be believed if it made a promise, whether or not the promise could be legally enforced.

It initially appeared that the final project required no zoning relief. A city planning official initially misread the code, however, and a small, noncontroversial special permit was required, which illustrates an important point in connection with negotiated zoning approvals. A project's attorney should always be certain he can deliver a supportive opinion concerning the project's legality to the lender. Sometimes local municipalities, far from fighting, become so friendly they give permits that could not withstand legal challenge.

Notwithstanding the absence of zoning relief, however, certain other discretionary acts were required of the town. The project required the abandonment of a road and other roads widened. The two major developers paid for them. The developers needed a permit to tear down two old buildings that were located on the area where a park would be located. (The park was a negotiated amenity, placed where the entrance to the project had originally been located. Residents wanted the entrance on the commercial side of the project to keep cars off local streets, but they also wanted a park. Hence, the developer and the residents compromised on the location.)

In connection with the application for a building permit, Hines needed a permit from the Cambridge Historical Commission to tear down a building that was more than 50 years old. The executive director of the commission assured Hines there would be no problem, and the neighbors and the city signed off on the project. When the hearing for the demolition permit was held, however, an unarmed lawyer sent to the hearing found 200 outraged neighbors. Although they wanted a park, they said, they were unaware Hines wanted to tear down the buildings to have a park.

The buildings are there today because the project was redesigned. As it turns out, it was probably one of the best decisions made. It does not make a lot of economic sense, but the two buildings that were there have been renovated, and Harvard is constructing a third building, a replica of buildings of that historic area. The buildings will be linked by a historic garden. It will be the new entranceway to the condominiums, and it has become a selling point for the project.

Keeping the neighbors involved was the key to the project's success. The time from Harvard's naming Hines as the developer for the project to the point when Hines received the building permit was approximately one year, an unusually short time for Cambridge.

Conclusion

In summary, a project such as University Place has three basic prerequisites to ensure successful negotiation of project approvals. First, to ensure credibility, the developer must do his homework to learn how a project will affect a particular site. Second, more homework is necessary to find problems that the town does not know it has. Third, it is important to document the results of negotiations in a way that ensures compliance of both the developer and the public entity. It is important to hire a good lawyer and make sure opinions supporting the agreement's legality and enforceability can be delivered.

CHAPTER 11
NEGOTIATING CONDITIONAL ZONING APPROVALS: MOUNT PROSPECT, ILLINOIS, AND MONTGOMERY COUNTY, MARYLAND
Joseph P. Clancy

Development issues are becoming even more localized. For many years, development and rezoning were "local issues" determined at the lowest level of government; county, city, and town councils and planning boards, since the advent of zoning, controlled the destinies of homeowners who wanted to build a garage within a set-back line and of regional mall developers seeking a new interchange on a federal highway. Now, however, civic associations, homeowners groups, condominium associations, and other local groups are being actively invited into the process. Rezoning and development approval required approval from local governing bodies, but now civic associations and residential groups are taking on a quasi-governmental authority. The more localized the decision-making authority becomes, the more issue-oriented it becomes. And the more localized it becomes, the more important it is to identify the issues early and confront them.

Two major rezonings provide classic examples of negotiating conditional zoning approvals--Mount Prospect, Illinois, and Montgomery County, Maryland. Originally, Opus Corporation entered into a venture to purchase, rezone, and develop a 300-acre parcel with single-family residential development on three sides into a business park in suburban Chicago. The property, located in an unincorporated area of Cook County, was zoned single-family residential. It was within the maximum expansion limits for annexation of Mount Prospect, and it was the municipality's intention pursuant to its master plan to allow business or industrial uses on the property. The other example is rezoning a 212-acre golf course along the I-270 corridor in Montgomery County, Maryland. The property is currently zoned for high-density residential, low-density residential, and relatively low-density business/commercial uses.

Joseph Clancy is senior vice president of Ackerman & Company, Gaithersburg, Maryland.

In entering a rezoning process, particularly for a large parcel that is likely to be controversial, it is important to identify the local issues as early as possible. The local issues in the Cook County property were design and density, for the Montgomery County project (known as the Washingtonian Center) transportation and traffic primarily and, secondarily, density and height. If transportation and traffic issues cannot be resolved, design and density issues become moot.

Mount Prospect, Illinois

When a developer approaches a piece of property requiring a zoning change, he must first identify the issues before entering into an agreement with the existing landowner or a financial partner or lender regarding purchase or development. The period of time necessary to rezone a piece of property is directly related to the difficulty of overcoming the primary issue or issues. In the Cook County project the issues were within the developer's control. If a project were well landscaped and planned so as not to take on the flavor of the traditional Chicago grid layout so common in that area's industrial parks--but to be more aesthetically pleasing and people oriented--the likelihood of success was high. On the other hand, if the project were designed with a floor area ratio that was too low, the economics would put the developer in an uncompetitive position. Homeowners' objections could be overcome by landscape design, architecture, and density; therefore, the issues were within the developer's control. The developer was able to negotiate an annexation agreement with the Village of Mount Prospect over the objections of many of the homeowners. The annexation agreement established the character of the design and plan and committed the developer to both.

Montgomery County, Maryland--Washingtonian Center

The Washingtonian Center in Montgomery County included three levels of transportation issues: site-localized transportation issues, area transportation issues, and regional transportation issues. Dealing with these transportation issues has involved a constant process of conversing with, negotiating with, and cajoling the State Highway Administration, the county Department of Transportation, the County Executive's staff, the County Council, the Planning Board and staff, homeowners' groups, and mayors, councils, and planning boards of the adjacent municipalities of Gaithersburg and Rockville.

Ackerman & Company, the developer, identified all three issues immediately and determined that it could work on the site-localized issues--those issues having to do with on-site traffic and the traffic immediately adjacent to the property--by entering into an agreement with the county with respect to roadways immediately adjacent to the property. Ackerman & Company was concerned, however, that it would be blamed for and held accountable for traffic problems that had nothing to do with the project. As a matter of fact, the cities of Gaithersburg and Rockville were already objecting to the areawide master plan being considered by the County Council and county Planning Board. Those two cities were critical, as they were immediately adjacent to the proposed project and were opposed to it.

The cities of Gaithersburg and Rockville and the citizens' associations in and around Gaithersburg and Rockville were not going to allow a master plan for the area nor this project to proceed until the areawide transportation problems were solved. By establishing a very positive and direct working relationship with the county's Department of Transportation, particularly its transportation planning group, the developer was able to encourage the problem-solving process. These efforts were aided by the county's own attempt to develop a business park in the general area and the county's need for significant improvement in areawide roads.

The most serious problem has been regional transportation, but it is enroute to being solved. A Metro rapid transit station recently opened within two miles of the project. The state and the county have agreed that a new intersection is required on I-270, the road immediately adjacent to the project where it has almost 5,000 feet of frontage. This new interchange from I-270 provides an opportunity to tie access into the interstate highway. Finally, the federal and state governments have determined that I-270 will be widened from a six-lane to a 12-lane highway and that a system of collector/distributor roads will be built.

To address the transportation issues related to Washingtonian Center, the developer hired a reputable transportation and traffic consulting firm to perform an exhaustive analysis of roadway systems and projected development in the surrounding area. It was told to incorporate all the transportation or road changes that were going to be made in the next 10 years and then assign to those roads all of the traffic generated from future development proposed in the area to see what the effects of traffic would be. The consulting firm was told to be conservative and to generate real numbers.

The intention was to produce a report that would be accurate, would stand up to partisan scrutiny, and could even be used in marketing to prospective tenants and users. The material was presented directly to the councils and planning boards of Gaithersburg and Rockville, which continued to oppose the project. In addition, the report was shared with interested citizens' groups. The press was advised about the transportation issue, the concerns, and the proposed solution. The developer stated that if the roads were not in place, the project would not proceed. This candid and accurate report and the developer's open approach were somewhat refreshing.

Open dialogue was the key to dealing with the mayors, city councils, planning boards, and civic associations. No one entity could solve the problems alone. Negotiation and approval are not completed. The municipalities of Gaithersburg and Rockville remain uncertain about the project. Some changes were made in an areawide master plan that was being considered, and those changes will tie development to roadway construction. The development can go ahead with a specific number of square feet only as contracts are let to build specific road sections.

The County Executive's Office has provided constant input, but the County Executive of Montgomery County has no official role to play in rezoning matters. He does control road construction, however, and the developer has been negotiating a public improvements agreement with the executive department for a year and a half. Ackerman & Company, on behalf of this project, will agree to provide a certain sum of money for off-site roads. The developer will give the county and state land and contribute money toward the interchange on I-270, which provides Washingtonian Center with direct access. A very expensive interchange has been designed to allow buildout of the project. In addition, the developer is engineering and designing roads that have little impact upon the project to advance the construction timeframe and to place the county and the state in a posture where they can have those roads built.

Conclusion

When an issue is identified, it is important to address it head on. Developers have nothing to sell but time. A developer, with a bag of money, is like a farmer with a bag of seeds. He walks from opportunity to opportunity and sprinkles some of that money on the land. He must be extremely careful which land he sprinkles the seeds on because some land is good and some is poor. The judgment a developer must make is how to spend his bag of seeds (or bag of money) so the bag grows rather than diminishes over time. In Montgomery County, Maryland, which has grown almost phenomenally in the last 10 years, particularly the last five, a developer is unwise to spend any of his seeds on situations where traffic and transportation issues cannot be resolved quickly. It is important to seek out those opportunities where a developer, by confronting issues head on, can be involved in their solution. With respect to the Washingtonian Center, Ackerman & Company has been part of the solution and has been one of the most aggressive elements that has encouraged a solution to the problems.

In addition, a developer cannot afford to be arrogant about the problems and the solutions. If approached and dealt with in a straightforward manner, homeowners' associations are often reasonable. They have agendas. If a developer can accept fallacies pointed out in his argument or can suggest alternatives and is willing to compromise, some degree of success is likely. To work solely through the public agencies and not communicate with the citizens' associations is usually a terrible mistake. The citizens' associations are the ones who will actively coalesce behind candidates, and the members of the municipal or county councils or planning boards are very much aware of that. Furthermore, dealing directly with the citizens and civic associations and discussing issues directly with them will sooner, rather than later, indicate to a developer whether or not he can overcome the problems. A developer must be certain that he is not spending his time on a project that is not going to proceed.

In summary, a developer has several axioms to work by: identify the issues, work closely with the local civic, community and homeowners' associations, understand the approval process to the extent necessary, and put all your energy and effort behind solving the issues perceived to be important to local associations and officials. Do not waste a lot of time with aesthetics or graphics or generalized concepts until you have identified local issues and solutions are under way.

SECTION 5

LEGAL ISSUES

Public/private negotiations and resultant agreements raise a number of legal issues and are constrained by recent legal cases. These legal issues are examined in detail by Katherine E. Stone and Cristina L. Sierra in "Case Law on Public/Private Written Agreements" and in a detailed outline, "Legal Constraints on Public/Private Negotiations," by Robert H. Freilich.

Chapter 12

CASE LAW ON PUBLIC/PRIVATE WRITTEN AGREEMENTS
Katherine E. Stone and Cristina L. Sierra

This chapter addresses unresolved legal questions that surround development agreements. When entering into development agreements, public and private interests should consider cases that provide some guidelines for drafting enforceable agreements. This chapter discusses a number of these cases from courts throughout the country.

Most development agreements attempt to create a vested right to complete construction of a development project, giving rise to the following major legal questions:

1. Does the agreement unlawfully contract away the reserved powers of the state?

2. Is the agreement a legislative, administrative, or adjudicatory act?

3. Does the agreement deprive nonparties of their due process rights to notice and hearing?

4. Is the agreement protected by the Contracts Clause of the United States Constitution?

A recent California Supreme Court case, Pardee Construction Company v. City of Camarillo, which involved a development agreement entered into by way of a stipulated judgment and illustrates the difficulty with attempting to vest development rights is also discussed. (A copy of the opinion is attached as an appendix to this chapter.)

Katherine E. Stone and Cristina L. Sierra are attorneys with Burke William & Sorensen, Los Angeles, California.

Vested Rights and Equitable Estoppel

A "vested right" to develop land usually means a right that is "secure, recognized or presently existing."[2] There is no consensus on the derivation of the so-called common law right to complete construction of a development project.[3] All jurisdictions seem to recognize that until vested, the right to develop land is always subject to legitimate police power qualifications. The jurisdictions differ, however, in their perception as to what point in the development process the right to complete construction vests. In pro-developer jurisdictions, the right will vest early in the process and be liberally construed.[4]

By contrast, a restrictive interpretation of vested rights is the California rule as stated by Justice Mosk in Avco Community Developers, Inc. v. South Coast Regional Commission:[5]

It has long been the rule in this state and in other jurisdictions that if a property owner has performed substantial work and incurred substantial liabilities in good faith reliance upon a permit issued by the government, he acquires a vested right to complete construction in accordance with the terms of the permit. Once a landowner has secured a vested right the government may not, by virtue of a change in the zoning laws, prohibit construction authorized by the permit upon which he relied.

At a very minimum, at least some type of final discretionary governmental approval, "which affords substantially the same specificity and definition to a project as a building permit" is clearly required.[6] While some California courts of appeal have suggested that the right to complete construction should rest upon final discretionary approval by the permitting agency,[7] the California Supreme Court has not taken the opportunity to retreat from Avco.[8] It was the harshness of California's late vesting rule that prompted the California legislature in 1979 to adopt legislation authorizing local governments to enter into development agreements.[9]

In their 1978 law review article, Cunningham and Kremer point out that although the vested rights rule is based on principles of equitable estoppel, courts have not generally engaged in an estoppel analysis to determine whether the right has vested. Instead, as in Avco, rigid rules specifying a particular point in the development process are applied,[10] notwithstanding the scope and duration of the project. For example, the same rule was applied to Avco's multiphased planned community with over $2 million in startup costs[11] as was applied to Santa Monica Pines's[12] conversion of a 42-unit apartment to condominiums with $1,700 invested.

Application of traditional rules of equitable estoppel might produce different results. Equitable estoppel may be invoked against the government where it will not "effectively nullify a strong rule of policy adopted for the benefit of the public" and where the following four elements are present:

1. The party to be estopped must be apprised of the facts;

2. He must intend that his conduct shall be acted upon;

3. The other party must be ignorant of the true state of facts; and

4. He must rely upon the conduct to his injury.[13]

Mayor and City Council of Baltimore v. Crane[14] is a classic example of the principle of estoppel's being used to enforce a development agreement against a city. The city of Baltimore, Maryland, enacted an ordinance that provided that where a property owner dedicated land to the city for street purposes, the property owner would be granted density benefits. The plaintiffs in that case made the necessary dedication but were later refused the density benefits by the planning commission on the ground that under the newly enacted zoning ordinance a conditional use permit was required for the development.

The court in Crane held that the case involved neither vested rights nor contract or conditional zoning because the ordinance was not enacted especially for the benefit of the plaintiffs but constituted rather an open-ended offer to any developer. The court held, however, that the plaintiffs, by dedicating property to the city, had acquired a vested contractual interest and that the city was estopped from enforcing its new zoning ordinance against them because of their substantial change in position, stating, "There is no question that the doctrine of equitable estoppel may be asserted against a municipal corporation in circumstances like those here....Indeed, where a municipal corporation has made an offer by ordinance which has been accepted and acted upon by another, a contract may arise, the obligation of which is constitutionally protected against impairment."[15]

For a development agreement to fulfill its primary objective (at least from a developer's point of view) of creating a vested right to develop, it should incorporate the rationale of the vested rights doctrine and principles of estoppel. For example:

1. The agreement should describe the development project with sufficient definition and specificity to meet the criteria of Avco.

2. All discretionary permits should be obtained before or at the time the agreement is approved.

3. The public policies promoted by the agreement should be specified in the agreement.

4. The developer's reliance on the agreement should be detailed.

Even if the agreement is insufficient to create a vested right, reliance on the agreement may be sufficient to invoke the doctrine of equitable estoppel.

Does the Agreement Unlawfully Contract Away the Reserved Powers of the State?

The most difficult legal hurdle confronting the validity of development agreements is the argument that the governmental agency, by entering into the agreement, has contracted away its power to protect the health, safety, and welfare of the public. The United States Supreme Court in Allied Structural Steel Co. v. Spannaus[16] defined this power as follows:

> This power, which in its various ramifications is known as the police power, is an exercise of the sovereign right of the Government to protect the lives, health, morals, comfort and general welfare of the people, and is paramount to any rights under contracts between individuals.[17]

As early as 1880, the United States Supreme Court in Stone v. Mississippi[18] enunciated the well-established rule that a governmental entity cannot contract away its right to exercise the police power. Hence, this police power and the prohibition against contracting it away have been termed the "reserved powers doctrine."

102

Courts throughout the country rely upon the reserved powers doctrine as a basis for invalidating governmental actions purporting to relinquish the power of the governmental agency to take future actions, if deemed necessary, to protect the general welfare of the public. In _Avco_,[19] for example, a developer sought to escape the imposition of certain permit requirements imposed under the California Coastal Zone Conservation Act on its development by alleging that it had previously entered into a state-approved agreement with the Orange County Harbor District pursuant to which Avco would, among other things, sell the county property below fair market value in exchange for favorable zoning and land use approvals. Based upon this agreement, Avco argued that the state was estopped from imposing further land use conditions upon its rights to build. The California Supreme Court rejected this estoppel argument, stating:

> Land use regulations...involve the exercise of the State's police power and it is settled that the government may not contract away its right to exercise its police power in the future. Thus, even upon the dubious assumption that the Beach Agreement constituted a promise by the government that zoning laws thereafter enacted would not be applicable to [Avco's property], the agreement would be invalid and unenforceable as contrary to public policy.[20]

Courts in other jurisdictions have similarly applied the reserved powers doctrine under various circumstances involving agreements between public entities and landowners that purport to "contract away" the state's police power.[21]

The effect of the reserved powers rule is to invalidate contracts that amount to a "surrender" or "abnegation" of control of a governmental entity's police power.[22] The mere fact that an agreement may have the effect of binding the legislative body beyond the terms of the individual legislators who approve and execute the agreement, however, does not necessarily amount to a surrender of that control. Thus, the key to a valid development agreement is one that reserves to the governmental entity the ability to control the development in accordance with applicable state and local regulations. Various provisions may be included in these agreements to accomplish this result.

The California Development Agreement Statute, for example, specifies that the agreement must set forth the duration of the agreement.[23] Thus, an agreement enacted pursuant to this law, or any agreement incorporating a definite period of duration, by its own terms, indicates that the state has not completely surrendered control of the police power.

The California Development Agreement Statute also provides for, and requires, municipalities or counties entering into agreements to monitor the developer's adherence to the terms of the agreement if the developer breaches the agreement.[24] The public entity is also authorized to modify or suspend provisions of the agreement if state and federal law enacted subsequent to the agreement precludes compliance with such provisions.[25] These provisions of the California statute are intended to ensure that control of the police power has not been contracted away. Similar provisions should be incorporated into development agreements in states that do not have statutes authorizing development agreements.

An additional precaution that should be taken when drafting and/or executing development agreements is to make sure that all discretionary approvals required for the development have been granted before the execution of the agreement (e.g., conditional use permits, zone changes), or, if they cannot be granted before execution of the agreement, to insert a provision in the development agreement stating that all future land use entitlements not yet granted must be obtained in accordance with all applicable state and local regulations.

State v. City of Spokane[26] illustrates the wisdom of such precautions. In that Washington case, a challenge was brought against an agreement entered into between the city and a developer based upon an alleged agreement by the city to vacate certain streets on land to be acquired by the developer. Although the court found that the challenged provision did not constitute an agreement by the city to vacate the streets, the court said that such an agreement would be ultra vires and void because street vacation, under state law, can be accomplished only upon the grant of a petition for the same by the legislative body after it determines the merits of the petition and weighs all the evidence presented by both the proponents and the objectors.[27] In other words, the court held that the city could not contract away the right to exercise its discretion as required by statute.

Similarly, in Morrison Homes Corp. v. City of Pleasanton,[28] the California court pointed to a provision in an annexation agreement at issue that stated the land would be developed in accordance with the city's "master plan and ordinances" as evidence that control of the city's police powers had not been contracted away.[29]

Making sure that all discretionary approvals are granted before the execution of the development agreement and in accordance with all applicable laws may also avoid a challenge to the development agreement on the ground that the agreement constitutes "contract zoning," which is nothing more than a challenge based upon the reserved powers doctrine. "Contract zoning has been described as an agreement which purports to bind both the landowners and the local government agency to an agreed set of covenants."[30] When a development agreement obligates the governmental entity to grant a zoning or other land use approval, the agreement is fair game for a challenge based upon the reserved powers doctrine.

In a New Jersey case, V.F. Zahodiakin Corp. v. Zoning Board of Adjustment,[31] the court refused to enforce a contract between a landowner and the city in which the city agreed to grant the landowner a variance to improve his property, stating that basic legislative functions could not be surrendered or curtailed by bargain or contract.[32]

The reserved powers doctrine was invoked in a Texas case, Hartnett v. Austin,[33] where the court refused to permit property to be rezoned solely on the ground that in exchange for the rezoning the zoning applicant had agreed to comply with certain land use restrictions. The court in Hartnett stated that the city could not contract away its police power and that the rezoning would have to be based upon a proper ground to be valid.[34] On the other hand, in one New York case, Church v. Town of Islip,[35] the court refused to use the reserved powers doctrine to invalidate rezoning granted by the municipality in exchange for the agreement by the landowner to adhere to certain development conditions and restrictions. The court in Town of Islip agreed that contract zoning was invalid as a legislative body cannot bargain away or sell its powers. In effect, however, the court brushed aside the reserved powers argument by stating, "We deal here with actualities, not phrases." Upon finding that the conditions or covenants imposed upon the property owner were in all respects lawful, the court refused to hold that the agreement violated the reserved powers doctrine.[36]

In Kings Mill Homeowners v. Westminister,[37] the Colorado court held that a zoning ordinance contingent upon a property's being developed, within a certain period of time, into a regional shopping center did not violate the reserved powers doctrine, stating, "The conditions were imposed to meet increasing need caused by the great population expansion in the area and at the same time to make the change from residential to commercial use a smooth transition."[38]

Although the cases on "contract zoning" may not be directly on all fours with situations involving development agreements, they do suggest that discretionary approvals should be granted in accordance with applicable regulations and not in exchange for benefits from developers to avoid the "reserved powers" challenge.[39]

The authorization provided by the California Development Agreement Statute[40] provides an example of another argument that development agreements do not violate the reserved powers doctrine. The public entities to which the statute applies are authorized by state law to enter into development agreements in the exercise of their police powers, and, in so doing, they are acting as agents of the state to further the state purposes and objectives set forth in the Development Agreement Statute. Therefore, the argument goes, the grant of authority and power to execute development agreements by the state under its police power contemplates performance of the agreement, and the local entity has no authority to breach it.

This rationale for upholding a statutorily authorized development agreement was used by the court in Housing Authority v. City of Los Angeles.[41] In that case, the court refused to invalidate a cooperation agreement between the parties that required the city to vacate certain roads, streets, and alleys and rezone certain property to allow for development of a low-rent housing project. The court rejected the city's argument that it had the power to rescind the contract as an invalid attempt to bind itself as to government functions, holding:

[T]he cooperation agreement is not an unauthorized attempt by the city to bind itself as to the exercise of governmental functions. It is simply an authorized contract to cooperate in the performance of those functions and as such is valid. Thus, control of city streets is a governmental function which the city without authority may not by contract prohibit or curtail. But as pointed out the city is authorized under the state law to cooperate by contract with the housing authority in the exercise of the granted power to close city streets, and in doing so is acting pursuant to the statute in a matter of state concern. In this as in the other respects the general principle applies that the state grant of the powers and the authority to execute and enter into the contract to exercise those powers contemplates performance of the contract and implies no authority to breach it.[42]

Incorporating a provision in development agreements that sets forth some state legislative authority for executing the agreement would help support the validity of the agreement. Although California is the only state that presently has a development agreement statute, other statutory sources of authority have been enacted in other states for agreements that are, in effect, development agreements.[43]

Notwithstanding the reserved powers doctrine and California's restrictive rules, the following California cases illustrate how courts have upheld development agreements as valid exercises of police power.

In Carruth v. City of Madera,[44] the court upheld an annexation agreement wherein the city agreed to install and pay for certain subdivision agreements upon approval of the subdivision plan and annexation of the property within the subdivision. The city, several years after entering into the agreement, had refused to install the improvements, claiming that the contract was invalid because it deprived future city councils of the right or power to determine city policy and public need relative to annexation of property. The court in Carruth rejected the city's argument, stating:

> The question is whether one council, in carrying out a necessary power, can make a contract similar to the one here, that binds its successors. Any doubt on this point was set at rest by the Supreme Court in Denio v. City of Huntington Beach, 22 Cal.2d 580, at page 590 [140 P.2d 392]: "It is our opinion, however, that the law is settled in California that a contract made by the council or other governing body of a municipality, which contract appears to have been fair, just, and reasonable at the time of its execution, and prompted by the necessities of the situation or in its nature advantageous to the municipality at the time it was entered into, is neither void nor voidable merely because some of its executory features may extend beyond the terms of office of the members of such body. In the absence of some other ground of avoidance, such a contract is binding upon the municipality and may not be summarily canceled by a successor council."[45]

The key in Carruth is that the agreement must be fair, just, and reasonable and in its nature advantageous to the public entity.

In Morrison Homes Corporation v. City of Pleasanton,[46] the court upheld a series of annexation agreements entered into by and between the city and a developer that provided, among other things, that the city would annex certain property and zone the property to allow the developer's proposed development. The developer agreed to construct both on- and off-site improvements that would tie into the city's water supply, sewer disposal, and storm drainage systems. Amendments to the agreements assured to the developer sufficient capacity in the city's sewer treatment facilities to serve the development. After the property was annexed and developed as agreed, the city was issued a cease and desist order from the Regional Water Quality Control Board prohibiting new connections to the city's sewer treatment plant. The city discontinued the connections to the developer's property, and the developer brought suit to enforce the agreements.

The court in Morrison Homes rejected the city's argument that the agreements were unenforceable as an invalid attempt to contract away the legislative and governmental functions of future city councils. Instead, the court acknowledged the general rule that a municipality may not contract away these functions but held that the effect of the rule is to void only those contracts that amount to a city's "surrender" or "abnegation" of its control of a properly municipal function.[47] Additionally, provisions in the agreements, such as the requirement that the property be developed in accordance with the city's master plan and ordinances, were, according to the court, in fact evidence of the city's reservation of control over the subject property. Therefore, the city had not surrendered control of its police power.[48] The court found further that the agreements were "just, reasonable, fair and equitable" as of the time they were executed and thus could not be avoided solely on the ground that some of their executory features might extend beyond the terms of the then City Council members.[49]

Most recently, in M.J. Brock & Sons, Inc. v. City of Davis,[50] a developer sought to enforce an agreement entered into between the city of Davis, California, and the developer's predecessor in interest wherein the city had agreed to zone the subject property to allow development of the property for urban uses in accordance with the general plan in exchange for the property owner's consent to annexation. The plaintiff, having commenced negotiations for the purchase of the property, met with city representatives, who ratified and affirmed the prior actions in connection with the original owner.

After the plaintiff had purchased the property and spent considerable sums of money on drainage studies at the request of the

108

city, the city rezoned the property, the effect of which was to preclude the development proposed by the plantiff. The plantiff brought an inverse condemnation action in the Federal District Court for damages alleged to be the fair market value of the property. The Federal District Court, without deciding the case on the merits, stated:

> Although zoning itself is not a contractual act, a municipality should not be allowed to avoid responsibility for breach of specific land use agreements entered into with private parties even though the breach occurred through the process of zoning changes.[51]

Other jurisdictions have used various rationales to uphold agreements that are tantamount to development agreements. In _Mayor and City of Baltimore_ v. _Crane_,[52] discussed previously, the city of Baltimore, Maryland, enacted an ordinance providing that where a property owner dedicated land to the city for street purposes, the property owner would be granted density benefits. When the city refused to grant the density benefits to the developer, the court held that the developer, by dedicating property to the city, had acquired a vested contractual interest and that the city was therefore estopped from enforcing the new ordinance against the developer.[53]

In _Meegan_ v. _Village of Tinley Park_,[54] the Illinois court held an annexation agreement unenforceable solely on the ground that the duration of the agreement as provided by statute had expired. The court stated, however, that, "[a]s long as the annexation agreement was in effect, the parties with a right to enforce the agreement could have done so and their rights would not have been curtailed or impaired by the amendment to the zoning ordinance [which, in effect, precluded the proposed development]."[55]

Broward County v. _Griffey_,[56] a Florida case, involved a zone change granted by the county to a landowner and a landowner's agreement to deed property within the area to be rezoned to the county for building a road. The court rejected the argument that the county had bargained away its police powers, stating that no private contracts were involved and that, "[t]here was no showing the county exacted anything from the Griffeys other than would be required of any R-4A zoning classification."[57]

Bracey v. _Long Branch_,[58] a New Jersey case, involved a cooperation agreement between a city and a local housing authority. The agreement provided in part that the city would amend the zoning map to allow for a housing program. The court rejected the argument that the agreement unlawfully contracted away the city's police powers on the ground that the agreement was authorized by state law and therefore an ordinance effectuating the agreement was a proper exercise of the city's zoning power.[59]

In _Herr_ v. _City of St. Petersburg_,[60] a suit based upon the reserved powers doctrine was brought to invalidate a settlement agreement entered into between a railroad company and the city of St. Petersburg, Florida, in which the railroad company agreed to relocate its facilities and convey the property upon which the facilities were then located to the city, and the city agreed to acquire other property and construct the new depot. The court, at the outset, pointed out the public interest in relocating the depot. As to the reserved powers argument, the court stated:

> Obviously, the city cannot by this contract bind future council in respect to the exercise of the police power or bargain away this prerogative of government. But we see no reason to vitiate the contract because of the covenants of the city, made therein, to do what would necessarily be its duty, with or without such covenants, in order to effectuate the comprehensive overall plan agreed upon between the parties to accomplish the municipal purposes to be achieved thereby.[61]

In a Colorado case, _Kings Mill Homeowners_ v. _Westminister_,[62] discussed earlier, the court upheld an agreement whereby the city agreed to rezone property and the developer agreed to develop it with a regional shopping center, stating that the agreement (or the conditions imposed on the rezoning) were necessary to meet the needs caused by increased population in the area and to make a smooth transition from the residential to commercial use of the property.[63]

In summary, the cases discussed in this section suggest guidelines that will increase the likelihood of a development agreement's being valid and enforceable:

1. Limit the agreement to a specific duration in time.

2. Require conformity to all subsequently enacted local regulations that are not inconsistent with the terms of the agreement.

3. Require that all discretionary approvals be obtained before execution of the agreement or insert a provision in the agreement that such entitlements shall be obtained in accordance with all applicable laws.

4. Recite whatever statutory authorization for the agreement may exist.

5. Recite the specific public benefits (e.g., the consideration, beyond that which can be exacted from the developer, to the public agency in exchange for the relinquishment of public powers).

6. Insert a provision requiring the governmental entity to monitor the developer's compliance with the agreement and allowing the government to terminate the agreement if the developer fails to comply.

Is the Agreement a Legislative, Administrative, or Adjudicatory Act?

Who cares whether a development agreement is a legislative, administrative, or adjudicatory act? The consequences that flow from the niceities of these distinctions are significant to the parties and should be kept in mind when drafting agreements. For example:

1. If the agreement is _legislative_, it is subject to initiative and referendum. Does this mean that the electorate can adopt a development agreement? California Government Code Section 65867.5 provides that, "[a] development agreement is a legislative act." But the courts have always considered it their province to decide the character of government activities.[64] Further, if the agreement is legislative:

a. It is subject to lesser judicial scrutiny;[65]

b. Its meaning is a question of law[66] and the intent of the drafters is irrelevant;[67] and

c. Notice and hearing are not required before approval.[68]

Legislative acts, however, are normally broad and establish public policy.[69] Development agreements do not seem to fit the category except insofar as they constitute zoning agreements.[70] If a development agreement is legislative, the problems discussed _supra_ are encountered because the agreement might be construed as an abdication of government's duty to govern.

2. If the agreement is administrative, it implements, rather than establishes, public policy.[71] Most public contracts are administrative and entered into pursuant to specific legislative authority. The ordinary rules governing awards of government contracts (e.g., bidding procedures) apply to administrative acts. Government contracts are protected by the Contracts Clause of the United States Constitution.[72] When governments seek to repudiate their contracts, they are subject to a higher degree of scrutiny under the Contracts Clause.[73]

3. If the agreement is adjudicatory, affected persons are entitled to due process. And findings based on substantial evidence are required to be made.[74]

The enforceability of a development agreement can be maximized if these fundamental distinctions in governmental actions are kept in mind. For example, the basic policy decisions should be in place before the agreement is adopted (i.e., the general plan and zoning should be adopted first). The agreement implementing these basic policies should be based on whatever statutory authority is available. The agreement should be treated as a judicial act, with findings recorded and more than adequate notice provided. Further, the agreement should be validated in a judicial proceeding.

Finally, the parties must remember it is a contract. Consideration flowing to the public body should be more than could be exacted under the police power.

Does the Agreement Deprive Nonparties of Their Due Process Rights to Notice and Hearing?

In Horn v. County of Ventura,[75] the California Supreme Court held that persons affected by adjudicatory land use decisions (such as subdivision approvals, conditional use permits, and variances) have a constitutional right to notice and an opportunity to be heard before the governmental approval. The notice must be adequate. That is, the notice, "must, at a minimum, be reasonably calculated to afford affected persons the realistic opportunity to protect their interests."[76] Notice provided by environmental review, for example, is not sufficient because, as stated in Horn:

[B]y limiting itself to the posting of environmental documents at central public buildings, and mailings of notices to those persons who specifically request it, the county has manifestly placed the burden of obtaining notice solely on the concerned individuals themselves. While such posting and mailing may well suffice to encourage the generalized public participation in the environmental decision making contemplated by [the California Environmental Quality Act], they are inadequate to meet due process standards where fundamental interests are substantially affected.[77]

The hearing must be meaningful. That is, it must be held at a meaningful point in the approval process, not, for example, after the decision has been made. Additionally, the hearing must be such that an affected landowner may have the opportunity to raise specific objections.[78] The principles of the <u>Horn</u> case, adequate notice and a meaningful opportunity to be heard, should be considered when entering into development agreements. The consequences of failing to do so could result in a void agreement.

Relying on <u>Horn</u>, several trial courts in California have held unconstitutional a California statute purporting to create a vested right to complete a development project. In <u>Palmer</u> v. <u>Ojai</u>,[79] the trial court held unconstitutional California Government Code Section 65956, which states in relevant part:

In the event that a lead agency or a responsible agency fails to act to approve or to disapprove a development project within the time limits required by this article, such failure to act shall be deemed approval of the development project.

The basis for the court's ruling was that Section 65956 does not afford persons affected by the project notice an opportunity to be heard before the "deemed approval." In <u>Palmer</u>, several hearings had been held before an environmental review board on the environmental impact report but no hearings before the decision-making body on the adjudicatory approvals that would be deemed approved under Section 65956.

Approval of a development agreement will normally be subjected to public hearing before approval by the public agency. For example, California Government Code Section 65867 requires hearings before both the advisory agency and the decision-making body before a development agreement may be executed. If no public hearing is held, the agreement will likely be void. But even if a hearing is held, the hearing notice may not be adequate, especially if the agreement has adjudicatory aspects. Adjudicatory decisions normally require more efforts to locate affected persons (e.g., mailing notice to residents within 300 yards) than do legislative decisions. As discussed previously, most development agreements are narrow and specific rather than broad and public, resembling more closely adjudicatory than legislative acts (notwithstanding California Government Code Section 65867.5, which states, in part, that "[a] development agreement is a legislative act").

Even if the agreement is legislative, the notice may be inadequate for purposes of apprising affected persons of the existence of the agreement and its impacts if the project description is not sufficiently definite. In Avco,[80] the court characterized permits granted pursuant to final adjudicatory action by the legislative body (e.g., conditional use permits) as those that "afford substantially the same specificity and definition to a project as a building permit."[81] It is suggested that this specificity and definition are essential elements in assuring adequate notice to affected persons.

In no event should a development agreement provide that the local agency will grant further discretionary approvals that normally require a public hearing (e.g., variances, conditional use permits, subdivision maps). Any hearing held on the further discretionary approvals, in such a case, would not be meaningful because the effect of the proviso would be to transform the approval from a discretionary act involving the due process principles of Horn to a ministerial act requiring the local agency to grant the approvals, regardless of the effect on adjacent landowners.

The questions raised by Horn can be avoided by:

1. Processing all discretionary permits before or simultaneously with the development agreement; or

2. Providing that the development agreement does not become fully operative until all discretionary permits for the project are approved; and

3. Providing maximum notice; and

4. Providing a very specific project description.

114

Is the Agreement Protected by the Contracts Clause of the United States Constitution?

Article I, §10 of the United States Constitution provides, in relevant part, "No State shall...pass any...Law Impairing the Obligation of Contracts." In U.S. Trust Co. v. New Jersey,[82] the United States Supreme Court made it clear that the Contracts Clause limits the power of states to modify their own contracts.[83] In that case, the states of New York and New Jersey entered into a statutory covenant relating to the uses that could be made of the funds of the New York and New Jersey Port Authority. The states agreed that so long as bonds were outstanding, the Port Authority could not, as a general rule, use funds that would be used to satisfy the bond indebtedness without first obtaining the bondholders' consent. The state of New Jersey repealed its statute and the bondholders brought suit, claiming that the statutory repeal constituted an impairment of the contract between the bondholders and the Port Authority.

The Supreme Court in U.S. Trust commenced its analysis by inquiring whether the contract between the states was one that bargained away the state's police power. The Court expressly held that the Contracts Clause did not require states to adhere to such contracts.[84] It did not end its analysis there, however, but instead found that the state action at issue involved the state's spending power about which the state could lawfully contract, notwithstanding the fact that the state was attempting to justify its action as one taken to protect the general welfare of the public.

The next step in the Court's analysis was to determine whether the state action in repealing the covenant "impaired" the contract between the Port Authority and the bondholders. Once it was determined that the contract had been impaired,[85] the Court proceeded to set forth the standard by which to determine whether such impairment constituted a violation of the Contracts Clause: state action impairing a contract will not violate the Contracts Clause if the action is both reasonable and necessary to serve an important public interest.[86]

The Court in U.S. Trust held the state to a stricter standard than the usual "rational basis" test typically used to review legislative actions not involving fundamental rights, stating that where the state itself is a party to the contract, complete deference to the legislative assessment of the reasonableness and necessity is inappropriate because the state's self-interest is at stake.[87] The Court found that the state's repeal of the covenant did violate the Contracts Clause because the bondholders' security was impaired by the action and because the action was not necessary to achieve the legitimate public interests that the state claimed the action was meant to further.[88] The Court stated that the state could achieve its goals by less drastic means, adding that under the stricter standard of review, the state was not free to exercise its legislative discretion to choose among alternatives.[89]

The Supreme Court again used the standard set forth in U.S. Trust in Allied Structural Steel Co. v. Spannaus.[90] In that case, however, the Court stated that the Contracts Clause, if it is to retain any meaning at all, must be understood to impose some limitations upon the ability of the state to impair contractual relationships between parties, even in the exercise of its legitimate police power.[91] Further, the Court stated that the greater the impairment, the closer the scrutiny of the state action.[92] In Allied Structural Steel, the state attempted to impose upon certain corporations a pension obligation beyond that which it had voluntarily agreed to undertake. The Court held that such action violated the Contracts Clause because of the substantial economic burden imposed on the corporations without any showing that this burden was necessary to meet an important general social problem.[93] The Court emphasized, in holding that the legislation did violate the Contracts Clause, its determination that the legislation had an extremely narrow focus and therefore could not be characterized as a law enacted to protect a "broad social interest."[94]

It is important to point out that not every failure by a governmental entity to perform under a contract constitutes an impairment of the contract. If the action of the state does not preclude a damage remedy, the action constitutes merely a breach of contract and the nonbreaching party can be made whole. If the governmental entity takes action that makes performance of the contract illegal or impossible, however, the nonbreaching party cannot be made whole because the governmental action would constitute a complete defense to an action for damages. In such a situation, the governmental action would constitute an impairment of contract, thus invoking the standard enunciated in U.S. Trust.[95]

The distinction between a breach of contract and an impairment of contract in the context of a development agreement is illustrated in E&E Hauling, Inc. v. Forest Preserve District, Etc.[96] In that case, the plaintiff entered into an agreement with the Forest Preserve District pursuant to which the plaintiff was given the exclusive right to operate a landfill at a recreational preserve. In exchange for this privilege, the plaintiff agreed to construct two scenic and recreational hills. The agreement did not restrict the materials that could be deposited in the landfill. Thereafter, the district adopted an ordinance prohibiting the dumping of liquid or sewage sludge at the landfill except septic tank dumpings and enforced this ordinance by stationing guards at the landfills who turned away trucks containing the prohibited materials under threat of arrest.

The court in E&E Hauling held that the action of the district in prohibiting the dumping pursuant to its legislative authority constituted a prima facie impairment of contract, subjecting the action to review under the standard set forth in U.S. Trust.[97] In making this determination, the court pointed out that if the plaintiff sued to enforce the contract, the district could claim the ordinance prohibited it from accepting the sludge, which claim would constitute a complete defense to the action. The plaintiff would be left with no remedy unless the ordinance was found to be invalid.[98]

These cases indicate that failure of the public entity, as a contracting party, to perform under a development agreement may subject it to a lawsuit for violation of the Contracts Clause if its failure is the result of legislative action that makes it illegal to perform. The public entity can defend its action and escape its obligations under the agreement only if it can establish that the action is both necessary (e.g., no less drastic alternatives are available that would achieve the same result) and reasonable to further an important public purpose (one that benefits the general public and not a small class of persons). Allied Structural Steel[99] is especially favorable to developers seeking to enforce development agreements under the Contracts Clause because that case held that increasing the financial burden on one of the contracting parties beyond that burden that it voluntarily agreed to undertake constituted a severe impairment requiring review under the Contracts Clause.[100]

It may be possible for the public entity to avoid the Contracts Clause problem by inserting a liquidated damages provision into the agreement with the proviso that both parties agree to pay these damages in the event that either party is unable, for any reason, to comply with the provisions of the agreement. The drawback to such a provision would be that the governmental entity may be unable to specifically enforce the agreement against a breaching developer.[101]

A liquidated damages provision may not be appealing to a developer simply because the reason a developer enters into development agreements--to determine vesting of development rights--would be frustrated if the government had the ability to destroy those vested rights by paying a predetermined amount of money as damages. Inclusion of a liquidated damages clause, however, if acceptable to the parties, would be evidence of the reservation by the government of control over its police powers and thereby avoid the "reserved powers" problems discussed _supra_.

Conclusion: A Case in Point

The principles of the cases discussed indicate that if a development agreement is to withstand judicial scrutiny, it must meet the following criteria:

1. It must not contract away all control of the public entity's police power. To avoid this fatal defect:

    a. The agreement should be limited to a specific time duration.
    b. The development project should be required to conform to all subsequently enacted local regulations not inconsistent with the terms of the agreement.
    c. All discretionary approvals should be obtained before the execution of the agreement, or, at a minimum, all land use entitlements sought subsequent to the execution that require discretionary approval should be obtained in accordance with all applicable laws.
    d. The agreement should set forth any statutory authorization for the agreement and the basic policy objectives of that authority the agreement is designed to accomplish.
    e. The specific public benefits to be gained by execution of the agreement beyond those that can be exacted from the developer without an agreement should be recited.
    f. Provision for a monitoring program by the public entity should be included to allow the public entity to terminate the agreement if the developer fails to comply.

2. It must not unconstitutionally infringe upon the rights of persons who are affected by the development. This situation may be avoided by treating the agreement as an adjudicatory act. As such, the following steps must be taken:

   a. Maximum notice must be provided, including a very specific project description.
   b. A full-blown hearing must be held before the execution of the agreement to give all affected persons the opportunity to voice their concerns over the development.
   c. Specific findings to support execution of the agreement must be provided.
   d. All discretionary approvals needed for the project must be granted pursuant to all applicable laws, including the requisite public hearing process.

As a final precautionary measure, the agreement should be validated in a judicial proceeding. If this step is to be taken, the agreement should contain a provision that the rights and obligations of the parties are contingent upon the validation of the agreement by judicial proceeding.

If a valid and enforceable development agreement is executed, the agreement will more than likely be protected by the Contracts Clause of the United States Constitution, the effect of which will be to prevent the public entity from taking any action that will constitute an impairment of the contract unless the public entity can meet the harsh standard of establishing that its action is both necessary and reasonable to further an important public interest.

Following the suggestions enumerated above will mean that the up-front costs for the developer will be far more substantial than if the developer were to proceed through the normal sequence of development approvals. The benefit, of course, is that once approved, a valid development agreement vests the right to complete the development, notwithstanding changes in applicable rules, regulations, and policies.

The reality is that more often than not, the courts have refused to construe a development agreement so as to override a change in public policy. A case in point is <u>Pardee Construction Company</u> v. <u>City of Camarillo</u>.[102]

119

Recently, the California Supreme Court in the case of Pardee
Construction Company v. City of Camarillo had an opportunity to
reconsider the vested rights rule set forth in its 1976 Avco decision.
The court was also presented with the question of whether a city may
contract away the police power by a consent judgment. Justice Mosk, (the
author of the Avco decision and the only justice remaining on the court
of those who decided Avco), along with Justice Bird, dissenting, opined
that reliance on the consent judgment resulted in a vested right. The
majority of the court did not reach the issues of vested rights or
contracting away the police power.

The facts that resulted in the controversy are classic. In the
spring of 1970, Pardee purchased about 1,150 acres of land in an
unincorporated area of Ventura County, adjacent to the city of Camarillo,
California. Pursuant to an annexation agreement, the city approved
Pardee's master plan for a phased, mixed-use development and zoned the
land to permit development in accordance with the master plan. In 1973,
after approving two of the subdivision maps and after Pardee had started
construction, the city downzoned the property to one unit per five acres.
Pardee filed a lawsuit that was resolved by a detailed stipulated
judgment, in the nature of a development agreement, entered July 1974.
The stipulated judgment provided that Pardee could proceed with the
development in accordance with its master plan and the previous zoning.

In 1981 the voters of the city adopted a growth control ordinance by
initiative. The growth control measure required residential developers
to compete for 400 annual development allotments and provided that no
building permit for nonexempted projects could be issued until an
allotment had been granted.[103]

Pardee contended that the ordinance was inconsistent with the
stipulated judgment and that it violated its vested right to proceed with
the development because under the ordinance it could be denied even one
building permit.

The majority of the court treated the consent judgment like a
contract but held that the growth control ordinance was not inconsistent
with the judgment because the growth control ordinance did not change
zoning or alter the master plan. The court held the growth control
ordinance is essentially a regulation of time or rate of development.[104]

Relying in part on a provision of the consent decree reserving to the city the police power to adopt and apply with an even hand ordinances that "may be applicable to all builders and developers alike through the City," the court held that: "As Pardee will compete with other builders, so will other builders have to compete with Pardee. Nothing in the judgment gives Pardee a monopoly on development in Camarillo."[105]

Justice Mosk (the author of Avco), dissenting, stated:

> The majority's interpretations of the consent judgment and the growth control ordinance are not merely unduly narrow, they are erroneous. As a consequence, Pardee is left without recourse to correct the blatant violation of its vested right to develop property in the manner guaranteed by the city. Indeed, after reviewing the conduct of the city, and the majority's approval thereof, one wonders whatever happened to vested property rights. If parties cannot rely on a stipulated judgment, there is no certainty in any document.[106]

The lesson for developers is to be sure the development agreement anticipates not only zone changes but other subsequent police power measures that could prevent development because, at least in California, the agreement will be narrowly construed.

The lesson for public agencies is that a reservation of the police power will be broadly construed to protect the public interest.

Notes

1   37 Cal.3d 465 (Dec. 6, 1984).
2   See Cunningham and Kremer, Vested Rights, Estoppel and the Land Development Process, 29 Hastings L.J. 625, 629 (1978).
3   See Cunningham, supra, for a discussion of the evolution of the vested rights rule and several vested rights rationales.
4   See Hagman, Estoppel and Vesting in the Age of Multi-Land Use Permits, 11 Southwestern University Law Review 545 (1979), for a discussion of pro-developer and anti-developer decisions from a number of jurisdictions.
5   17 Cal.3d 785, 791, 553 P.2d 546, 550, 132 Cal.Rptr. 386, 389 (1976).
6   Id. at 794.

7   Patterson v. Central Coast Regional Commission, 58 Cal.App.3d 833, 130 Cal.Rptr. 169 (1976).

8   See Santa Monica Pines Ltd. v. Rent Control Board, 35 Cal.3d 858, 201 Cal.Rptr. 593, 679 P.2d 27 (1984) and Pardee Construction Company v. City of Camarillo, 37 Cal.3d 465, _____ Cal.Rptr. _____, _____ P.2d _____ (Dec. 1984), two recent California Supreme Court decisions where the vested rights issue was not reached.

9   California Government Code Sections 65864-65869.5. Other vested rights legislation has been adopted by the California legislature. (See, e.g., Cal. Gov. Code §65956, vested map legislation.) See also Holliman, Development Agreements and Vested Rights in California, 13 Urban Lawyer 44 (1981).

10   See note 2, supra.

11   Avco, supra, at 790.

12   Santa Monica Pines, supra, at 861.

13   City of Long Beach v. Mansell, 3 Cal.3d 462, 493, 91 Cal.Rptr. 23, 476 P.2d 423 (1970).

14   277 Md. 198, 352 A.2d 786 (1976).

15   Id. at 790-91. See also Holliman, Development Agreements and Vested Rights in California, supra, 13 Urban Lawyer 44, 56 for an analysis of this case.

16   438 U.S. 234, 57 L.Ed.2d 727, 98 S.Ct. 2716 (1978).

17   Id. at 241.

18   101 U.S. 814.

19   17 Cal.3d 785.

20   Id. at 800. See also Scrutton v. County of Sacramento, 275 Cal.App.2d 412, 79 Cal.Rptr. 872 (1969); Call v. Feher, 93 Cal.App.3d 434, 444, 155 Cal.Rptr. 378 (1979).

21   See Carlino v. Whitpain Investors, 453 A.2d 1385 (Pa. 1982); V. F. Zahodiakin Corp. v. Zoning Board of Adjustment, 86 A.2d 127 (N.J. 1952); Hartnett v. Austin, 93 So.2d 86 (Fla. 1956); Hartman v. Buckson, 467 A.2d 694 (Del.Ch. 1983).

22   See Morrison Homes Corporation v. City of Pleasanton, 58 Cal.App.3d 724, 130 Cal.Rptr. 196 (1976).

23   California Government Code Section 65865.2.

24   Id. at Section 65865.1.

25   Id. at Section 65869.5.

26   422 P.2d 790 (1967).

27   Id. at 797.

28   58 Cal.App.3d at 724.

29   Id. at 734.

30 Kramer, Development Agreements: To What Extent Are They Enforceable? 10 Real Estate L.J. 29, 45 (1981).

31 86 A.2d 127.

32 Id. at 131-32.

33 93 So.2d 86.

34 Id. at 89.

35 203 N.Y.S.2d 866 (1960).

36 Id. at 867-68.

37 192 Colo. 305, 557 P.2d 1186 (Colo. 1976).

38 Id. at 312.

39 Other cases invalidating "contract zoning" have done so based on other grounds such as spot zoning, lack of enabling authority to contract zone, zoning for private as opposed to the public benefit, or failure to adhere to uniformity in application of zoning regulations. See Kramer, Development Agreements: To What Extent Are They Enforceable?, supra, 10 Real Estate L.J. at 46.

40 California Government Code Sections 65864 et seq.

41 38 Cal.2d 853, 243 P.2d 515 (1952).

42 Id. at 868. See also Holliman, Development Agreements and Vested Rights in California, supra, 13 Urban Lawyer 44, 57-58. In Palisades Properties, Inc. v. Brunetti, 44 N.J. 117, 133-34 (1965), the court held that a contract between a municipality and a charitable corporation had the effect of precluding a zone amendment by the city to increase the building height limitation but that the contract did not violate the reserved powers doctrine because the agreement was authorized by statute and its purpose was not to restrict the municipality from further zoning.

43 For example, annexation agreements are expressly authorized by statute in Illinois. (See Meegan v. Village of Tinley Park, 52 Ill.2d 354 (1972). Cooperation agreements between local governments and housing authorities are statutorily authorized in New Jersey. (See Bracey v. Long Branch, 73 N.J. Super. 91 (1972).) In both of these cases, the agreements contained provisions relating to zoning approvals, and in both cases the courts held the agreements to be valid exercises of the police power.

44 233 Cal.App.2d 688, 43 Cal.Rptr. 855 (1965).

45 Id. at 695.

46 58 Cal.App.3d 724.

47 Id. at 734.

48 Id.

49 Id. at 734-35. See also Denio v. City of Huntington Beach, 22
    Cal.2d 580, 140 P.2d 392 (1943), relied upon by the court in
    Morrison Homes. Denio involved a contract for legal services.
50 401 F.Supp. 354 (N.D.Calif. 1975).
51 Id. at 361.
52 352 A.2d 786.
53 Id. at 790.
54 52 Ill.2d 354.
55 Id. at 359.
56 366 So.2d 869 (Fla.App. 1979).
57 Id. at 871.
58 73 N.J. Super. 91.
59 Id. at 103-4.
60 114 So.2d 171 (Fla. 1959).
61 Id. at 175; cf. Hartman v. Buckson, 467 A.2d 694, 699, wherein the
    court held that a compromise agreement entered into between a city
    and a developer that allowed the developer an exception from open
    space development requirements was invalid, stating that the
    agreement bargained away the city's zoning power and holding that a
    city may not compromise claims arising out of a matter concerning
    which the city has no power to contract.
62 192 Colo. 305.
63 Id. at 312.
64 See e.g. Pacifica Corp. v. City of Camarillo, 149 Cal.App.3d 168,
    196 Cal.Rptr. 670 (1983).
65 Carty v. City of Ojai, 77 Cal.App.3d 329, 143 Cal.Rptr. 506 (1978).
66 Teachers Management & Invest. Corp. v. Santa Cruz, 64 Cal.App.3d
    438, 134 Cal.Rptr. 523 (1976).
67 County of Los Angeles v. Superior Court, 13 Cal.3d 721, 119
    Cal.Rptr. 631, 532 P.2d 495 (1975).
68 Horn v. County of Ventura, 24 Cal.3d 605, 613, 156 Cal.Rptr. 718,
    596 P.2d 1134 (1979).
69 Id.
70 See Arnel v. City of Costa Mesa, 28 Cal.3d 511, 169 Cal.Rptr. 904,
    620 P.2d 565 (1980), holding that a zoning ordinance, even if
    applicable to a small piece of property, is a legislative act.
71 Horn v. County of Ventura, supra, 24 Cal.3d 605, 613.
72 United States Trust Co. v. New Jersey, 431 U.S. 1, 17, 52 L.Ed.2d
    92, 97 S.Ct. 1505 (1977).
73 Id. at 26.
74 Topanga Assn. for a Scenic Community v. County of Los Angeles, 11
    Cal.3d 506, 113 Cal.Rptr. 836, 522 P.2d 12 (1974).

75 24 Cal.3d 605.

76 Id. at 617.

77 Id. at 617-18.

78 Id. at 619.

79 Case Nos. B003987 and B005635, appeal pending in California Court of Appeal, Second Appellate District.

80 17 Cal.3d 785.

81 Id. at 794.

82 431 U.S. 1, 52 L.Ed.2d 92, 97 S.Ct. 1505 (1977).

83 Id. at 17.

84 Id. at 23.

85 The court was clear in pointing out that not all impairments were sufficient to constitute a violation of the Contracts Clause. Id. at 21.

86 Id. at 26.

87 Id.

88 Id. at 19, 29-30.

89 Id. at 30-31.

90 438 U.S. 234, 57 L.Ed.2d 727, 98 S.Ct. 2716 (1978).

91 Id. at 242.

92 Id. at 245.

93 Id. at 245-47.

94 Id. at 248-49.

95 E&E Hauling, Inc. v. Forest Preserve District, Etc., 613 F.2d 675, 679 (1980), citing Hays v. Port of Seattle, 251 U.S. 233, 64 L.Ed. 243, 40 S.Ct. 125 (1920).

96 613 F.2d 675.

97 Id. at 680, 681.

98 Id. See also the discussion of Mayor and City Council of Baltimore v. Crane, supra, containing a quote from the court that the development agreement at issue was constitutionally protected against impairment.

99 438 U.S. 234.

100 Id. at 245-47.

101 Under the California Development Agreement statute, both parties may specifically enforce the agreement. California Government Code Section 65865.4.

102 37 Cal.3d 465.

103 Subsidized low-income and senior citizen housing and smaller developments were exempt from the ordinance (37 Cal.3d 465, 471).

104 Id. at 472.

105 Id. at 473.

106 Ibid.

APPENDIX

PARDEE CONSTRUCTION COMPANY v. CITY OF CAMARILLO

Summary

A city and a construction company entered into a consent judgment establishing the company's vested right to develop its property according to the master plan and the zoning ordinance in effect at the time development was begun. Subsequently, the city voters adopted an initiative measure establishing a growth control ordinance that regulated the rate of development in the city by limiting the number of dwelling units that could be built yearly. The trial court denied the construction company's request for a restraining order to enjoin the city from applying the growth control ordinance to the company's property. (Superior Court of Ventura County, No. 56637, Robert Lee Shaw, Judge.)

The Supreme Court affirmed, holding that the growth control ordinance validly applied to the construction company's property. Neither the judgment nor the master plan referred to any time schedule or rate of development, and the judgment reserved to the city the police power to adopt any ordinance, applicable to all developers, not inconsistent with the judgment. The growth control ordinance essentially regulated the rate of development but did not change the zoning or alter the master plan. Thus, it did not infringe on any of the construction company's rights under the judgment. (Opinion by Kaus, J., with Broussard, Reynoso, Grodin, and Lucas, J., concurring. Separate dissenting opinion by Mosk, J., with Bird, C.J., concurring.)

Opinion

Kaus, J. --Pardee Construction Company (Pardee) appeals from an order of the superior court denying Pardee's request for a "restraining order" to enjoin the City of Camarillo (the city) from applying a growth control ordinance (Camarillo Mun. Code, ch. 1, tit. 20 §§ 20.04-20.13) to Pardee's property. The question is whether application of the ordinance is precluded by an earlier consent judgment entered into between Pardee and the city.

In the spring of 1970, Pardee purchased about 1,150 acres in an unincorporated area of Ventura County, adjacent to the city. In the fall of 1970, the city approved Pardee's master plan for development of the property, annexed the property (Ord. No. 182) and zoned the property to permit development in accordance with the master plan (Ord. No. 178). The master plan, in Pardee's words, "(a) was a comprehensive plan for the development of the entire 1150 acres...(b) described in great detail the land use...and indicated the number of acres to be allocated to each type of development, the number of residential units...the other uses...such as parks, open spaces, schools, commercial and industrial, and the precise location of each such land use; (c) included a proposed zoning plan...(d) contained a generalized development proposal for the orderly and phased development of the entire 1150 acres...." The plan contained no time schedule, nor did it indicate the rate of development.

Pardee started to develop the property and built on it. As will be seen, progress was not without controversy. The proposed development plans for land use were subjected to what Pardee later described as "unreasonable conditions." Nevertheless, by the spring of 1973, the city had approved tentative and final subdivision maps for two tracts, Nos. 2189 and 2228, consisting of 71 acres and 325 residential lots, and construction had begun.

In the summer of 1973, the city adopted ordinances which contemplated changing the land use to reduce density--specifically, to provide that each residential unit occupy five acres. In 1974, Pardee brought suit praying for declaratory relief, damages, and an injunction. It also claimed inverse condemnation. The injunction and inverse condemnation causes of action were later dismissed by stipulation.

The focus of the complaint, contained in count I, was the city's proposed modification of land use to reduce density. It was alleged that the proposed new ordinance violated Pardee's vested right to proceed with the development of the property in accord with Ordinance No. 178--the zoning as promised at the time of annexation and adoption of the master plan. Count IV complained of the problems Pardee was having getting tentative tract maps approved and of the "arbitrary and capricious actions" on the part of$_2$ the city in approving Residential Planned Development (RPD) permits, in that the city was imposing frustrating new conditions, such as increase in footage of lots, houses, and yards, drainage and landscaping requirements, and contributions for road improvements. Pardee requested that the city be restrained from "abusing [its] administrative and legislative powers" to frustrate Pardee's plans to develop the property.

On July 11, 1974, Pardee and the city stipulated to a judgment which recited in paragraph 6 that because Pardee had incurred substantial expenses and obligations in reliance on the city's approval of its master plan, its assurances that Pardee could develop the property substantially in accordance with the plan, and its enactment of the zoning ordinance to permit the development, Pardee "has a vested right to proceed with the development of all of the Property$_3$ in the manner set out" in the master plan, as modified by the judgment, and that the city is "estopped from adopting zoning or permanent land use regulation for the Property which is in any manner inconsistent with" the master plan and the zoning ordinance which had been adopted$_4$ in accordance therewith except as expressly provided in the judgment.

The judgment provided in paragraph 19 that it did not preclude the city "in the proper exercise of its police power from adopting any ordinance which will be applicable to Pardee and the property so long as such ordinance is not inconsistent with the provisions of this judgment....It is the intent and purpose of the section that the City not be precluded from the exercise of its broad police power relative to general subject matter which may be$_5$ applicable to all builders and developers alike throughout the City."

Other pertinent paragraphs of the consent judgment confirm that the focus of Pardee's complaint and the judgment that followed was the dispute over land use and zoning, not the sequence and certainly not the timing of development. As noted earlier, paragraph 7 provided for modification of the master plan regarding residential development. Paragraphs 8 and 9 then provided that the land use element of the city's General Plan be made to conform to Ordinance No. 178 and that, pending amendment to the land use element of the General Plan, the city could not withhold conditional approval of any tentative tract map or RPD application solely on the ground that it did not conform to the General Plan, so long as it conformed to Ordinance No. 178. Paragraphs 10 and 11 provided for conveyance of more open space. Paragraphs 12, 13 and 14 provided for mobile home park, industrial tract, and school sites. Significantly, as to the mobile home park, the judgment provided that development of the park could proceed, "subject only to plaintiff's filing its application for a conditional use permit and its compliance with the development standards and individual site standards set forth in sections...of the Municipal Code."

Paragraph 15, an extensive paragraph dealing with the issuance of RPD permits, was clearly intended to alleviate the problems that had been described in count IV of the complaint. It provided that Pardee comply with all applicable provisions of the municipal code, city ordinances, and all other applicable requirements of law and that the city "shall not impose, except by duly enacted ordinance, any conditions or requirements for the issuance of permits for RPD developments"--except certain conditions set forth in an attached exhibit. The paragraph also precluded the city's planning commission from reviewing, changing, or modifying requirements or design criteria after approval by a city agency (i.e., city engineer or director of public works) having jurisdiction over the subject matter. Paragraph 16 dealt with tract map applications and RPD permits: it outlined the procedure for their processing, an important feature of which was the provision that, once an RPD permit was issued in compliance with all legal requirements, no further discretionary approval was necessary, although the developer still had to obtain a zoning clearance from the planning department and, of course, the requisite building permits. Finally, paragraph 17 provided for the issuance of use, building, and other permits upon request and compliance with "all legal requirements."

It is noted that the 1974 stipulated judgment resembled the 1970 master plan in its failure to contain any reference to a time schedule or rate of development.

In June 1981, the voters of the city adopted an initiative measure establishing a residential development control system (Growth Control Ordinance), which the city then enacted as sections 20.04 and 20.13 of its municipal code. The ordinance provided that from 1981 through 1995 the number of new residential units which could be built in the city was limited to 700 units in 1981 and 400 thereafter, subject to a 10 percent variance if authorized by the city council. Allocations for each year were to be established by the council after recommendation by a residential development control board on the basis of stated criteria.[6]

On July 7, 1981, a month after the initiative passed, in the same action in which the consent judgment was entered, Pardee filed a request for an order to show cause why application of the Growth Control

Ordinance should not be restrained as to Pardee. It alleged that the judgment established that it had a vested right to proceed with development according to its master plan and that the new ordinance could not, therefore, be applied to the development of the property that was the subject of the judgment.

On August 7, 1981, the parties filed a stipulation as to the issues to be decided on the order to show cause. These were: (1) the applicability of the Growth Control Ordinance to Pardee's property which was subject to the judgment of July 11, 1974; and (2) the alleged violation of a vested right granted to Pardee by that judgment. The validity of the Growth Control Ordinance was not put in issue.

The city's position in response to Pardee's request for an order to show cause was that the ordinance did not violate any vested right, but affected only the timing of development based on the criteria established in the ordinance; and, further, that the new ordinance came under the police power of the city, which had been specifically excluded from the operation of the judgment. A declaration by Matthew A. Boden, director of planning and community development for the city, stated that at no time previously had Pardee contended that the 1974 judgment prevented control of the rate of growth by the city.

The trial court, after a hearing on declarations, denied the application without opinion.

II

(1a) Pardee contends that application of the Growth Control Ordinance to its property deprives it of the vested right to develop the property, a right granted by the consent judgment.

(2) We first examine the judgment, keeping in mind that a consent judgment is in the nature of a contract (Stevens v. Stevens (1968) 268 Cal.App.2d 426, 435 [74 Cal. Rptr. 54]), subject to interpretation and construction. "It...is binding only as to the matter consented to by the stipulation...is confined only to issues within the stipulation...and does not cover matters not in the stipulation." (Rappenecker v. Sea-Land Service, Inc. (1979) 93 Cal.App.3d 256, [155 Cal.Rptr. 516])

(1b) The judgment here resulted from the dispute over the new zoning ordinance contemplated by the city which differed from that promised and enacted by the city upon the approval of a master plan.[8] As noted, the rate of development was in no way at issue in the litigation.

The judgment insured for Pardee the right to development of the property under a specific zoning ordinance. It did not set the timing or sequence of the development. (3) It did not exempt the development from compliance with the applicable municipal code and ordinances.[9] (1c) Further, by its express terms, the judgment reserves the police power to the city, providing that the city may adopt ordinances within the police power applicable to Pardee, so long as they are not inconsistent with the judgment.

The events giving rise to the judgment and the language of the judgment itself persuade us that, at most, Pardee was granted the right to develop its property in accord with the master plan and the zoning provided by Ordinance No. 178 and that the city, in turn, was estopped from adopting zoning or land use regulations for the property which were in any manner inconsistent with the plan for Ordinance No. 178.

The ordinance under attack is not in the least inconsistent with the consent judgment. It does not change the zoning provided by Ordinance No. 178; nor does it change any of the provisions of the master plan as modified by the judgment. It imposes no conditions, limitations or requirements on Pardee that are not "applicable to all builders and developers alike throughout the City," as stated in paragraph 19 of the judgment. The procedures for obtaining a residential development allotment and a building permit apply to Pardee as they do to any other developer.

The Growth Control Ordinance is essentially a regulation of the time, or rate, of development. It regulates the rate of development by limiting the number of dwelling units that may be built per year. It allocates the number of units among developers according to engineering and aesthetic criteria that, on their face, do not deprive Pardee of its right to build the units contemplated by the consent judgment. It does not change zoning and does not alter the master plan and therefore does not restrict or prevent Pardee from its development of the property in accordance with the master plan and the zoning provided by Ordinance No. 178.

Pardee argues that, even if no facial inconsistency between the judgment and the Growth Control Ordinance appears, the ordinance is

131

nevertheless inconsistent because, potentially, Pardee could be denied even one permit under the new ordinance. Pardee notes that the procedure for allocation of permits is based upon evaluations which take into consideration criteria that allow reevaluation of the merits of the project. Therefore, argues Pardee, its specifications regarding water and sewage capacities, and school and traffic capacities, for example—already approved under the master plan—will now have to compete with specifications of other builders so that, conceivably, Pardee may lose out to the extent of not getting a single permit. In essence, it urges that the city should not be permitted to evaluate Pardee's projects competitively for the purpose of deciding whether a permit should be granted. That argument ignores that portion of the judgment expressly reserving the police power to the city. The intent of that reservation was to insure that the city retained the power to adopt and apply with an even hand ordinances that "may be applicable to all builders and developers alike throughout the city." As Pardee will compete with other builders, so will other builders have to compete with Pardee. Nothing in the judgment gives Pardee a monopoly on development in Camarillo.

Since it is our view that the Growth Control Ordinance did not infringe on any of Pardee's rights under the 1974 judgment, it is irrelevant whether in some other context, they might be deemed "vested."

Broussard, J., Reynoso, J., Grodin, J., and Lucas, J., concurred.

Mosk, J.--I dissent.

The majority's interpretations of the consent judgment and the growth control ordinance are not merely unduly narrow, they are erroneous. As a consequence, Pardee is left without recourse to correct the blatant violation of its vested right to develop property in the manner guaranteed by the city. Indeed, after reviewing the conduct of the city, and the majority's approval thereof, one wonders whatever happened to vested property rights. If parties cannot rely on a stipulated judgment, there is no certainty in any document.

The Inconsistency between the Ordinance and the Judgment

The majority come to the conclusion that the growth ordinance does not run afoul of the stipulated judgment. They arrive at this strained interpretation by picking and choosing among the provisions of each to discern any compatible language. Essentially, the majority decided that the growth ordinance regulates only the timing of development, while the judgment relates exclusively to zoning. However, a more objective examination of both documents reveals obvious inconsistencies between the ordinance and the judgment.

The ordinance discloses on its face a purpose to affect more than the timing of development. Section 20.04(f) declares that "the City must be able to control the rate, distribution, quality and economic level of proposed development...." (Italics added) To achieve this control, the ordinance sets up a system whereby each developer must withstand extensive evaluation in order to obtain the allotments necessary for the issuance of building permits. (§§ 20.09 & 20.10) The evaluation procedure is decidedly substantive. Developers must compete in such areas as the capacity of proposed water, sewer and drainage systems, the ability of the fire department to serve the new area without building a new station, "the design quality" of the proposed buildings in terms of size, height, color, and location, and the amount of open space provided in the plan. (§§ 20.09A & 20.09B) If a developer does not obtain a certain number of "points," awarded by the residential development evaluation board, that developer will not be allowed a single allotment. Thus, based on the board's qualitative evaluation, a developer's project could be completely frozen until 1995. With inflation pushing labor and material costs higher each year, it is naive to conceive that such a substantive delay is only a matter of timing.

The majority's contention that the earlier judgment relates only to zoning, and not timing, overlooks the clear wording and intent of that document. A consent judgment is binding as to the issues in the stipulation. (Rappenecker v. Sea-Land Service, Inc. (1979) 93 Cal.App. 3d 256, 263 [155 Cal.Rptr. 516]) This does not mean, as the majority appear to believe, that only those issues in the underlying suit may be considered. It means that all subjects covered in the judgment are settled and binding as to the parties.

Paragraph 17 of the judgment provides that the city "shall issue to [Pardee] all necessary use, building and other permits and approvals, upon [Pardee's] request and compliance with all legal requirements...." Further, paragraph 19 declares that the city shall not be precluded "in the proper exercise of its police power from adopting any ordinance... so long as such ordinance is not inconsistent with the provisions of this judgment." (Italics added) It is patently obvious that the ordinance, which allows the city to deny Pardee any building permits until 1995, and the judgment, which provides that Pardee is entitled to all building permits it requires upon its request, are inconsistent. It is also clear that paragraph 19 of the judgment thus prevents the city from enforcing as to this plaintiff the very species of ordinance at issue in this case.

The majority attempt to limit the judgment to its effect on the city's power to change the zoning applicable to Pardee. But it is apparent that the judgment has a far broader purpose: i.e., to prevent the city from interfering in any significant way with Pardee's development plans. This broad purpose is manifested in paragraphs 17 and 18, which bear no relation to zoning. Paragraph 18 declares that the "City shall take no action which is inconsistent with the spirit and intent of the settlement agreement and this judgment." As quoted above, paragraph 17 requires the city to issue "all necessary use, building and other permits" to Pardee. Thus, city interference quite apart from zoning was considered by the parties and precluded by the judgment. The ordinance constitutes a direct violation of this mandate.[10]

The City's Preclusion from Interfering with Pardee's Vested Right

The city is precluded from applying the growth ordinance to Pardee not only by the express terms of the judgment, but also because the judgment gave Pardee a vested right to develop its property with which the city may not interfere. "It has long been the rule in this state and in other jurisdictions that if a property owner has performed substantial work and incurred substantial liabilities in good faith reliance upon a permit issued by the government, he acquires a vested right to complete construction in accordance with the terms of the permit." (Avco Community Developers, Inc. v. South Coast Regional Com. (1976) 17 Cal.3d. 785, 791 [132 Cal.Rptr. 386, 553 P.2d 546]) "'[T]he Legislature is without power to impair or destroy the obligations of contractual or vested rights....'" (Pardee Construction Co. v. California Coastal Com. (1979) 95 Cal.App.3d 471, 479 [157 Cal.Rptr. 184], quoting Estate of Thramm (1947) 80 Cal.App.2d 756, 765 [183 P.2d 97])

In the past, a developer had to obtain a building permit and expend substantial sums in reliance thereon in order to invoke the vested rights doctrine. But "[s]everal decisions intimate that a building permit may no longer be the sine qua non of a vested right if preliminary public

134

permits are sufficiently definitive and manifest all final discretionary approvals required for completion of specific buildings." (Raley v. California Tahoe Regional Planning Agency (1977) 68 Cal.App.3d 965, 975, fn. 5 [137 Cal.Rptr. 699]) "In determining which governmental permits other than a building permit may possibly afford the developer a vested right, some courts have applied the final discretionary approval test while others have disregarded whether the final act is discretionary or ministerial and simply looked to the final governmental approval." (Tosh v. California Coastal Com. (1979) 99 Cal.App.3d 388, 394 [160 Cal. Rptr. 170]; see also Avco Community Developers, Inc. v. South Coast Regional Community, supra 17 Cal.3d 785, 794; Billings v. California Coastal Com. (1980) 103 Cal.App.3d 729, 735 [153 Cal.Rptr. 288]; South Central Coast Regional Com. v. Charles A. Pratt Construction Co. (1982) 128 Cal.App.3d 830, 841-845 [180 Cal.Rptr. 555]; Aries Dev. Co. v. California Costal Zone Conservation Com. (1975) 48 Cal.App.3d 534, 544 [122 Cal. Rptr. 315])

Paragraph 17 of the judgment constitutes the city's guarantee that upon request Pardee will receive any permit--for building and all other purposes--necessary for the completion of the development. The wording of paragraph 17 makes clear the parties' intent to remove all discretion from the city by providing that the city "shall" issue all permits "upon [Pardee's] request." This guarantee--fully and fairly bargained for by parties in litigation--exemplifies governmental approval that is the equivalent of a building permit for the purpose of a vested rights inquiry. And plaintiff's good faith expenditure of over $13.5 million for onsite and offsite improvements, incurred in reliance on the judgment, finishes the inquiry. Since Pardee thus had a vested right to complete its development, the city could not interfere.

The order of the trial court should have been reversed, and the cause remanded with instructions to issue the restraining order as prayed, thus preventing the application of the ordinance to Pardee.

Bird, C.J., concurred.

Notes

1

The minute order dated August 29, 1981, states: "The above entitled matter having been heretofore heard and submitted to the court for consideration and decision; the court now orders the restraining order denied."

The proceedings which led to the order were instituted by the issuance of an order directing the city to show cause why it should not be "enjoined, restrained, and prohibited" from applying its ordinance to Pardee. No judgment was entered, but an order refusing to grant an injunction is appealable (Code Civ. Proc., §904.1 subd. (f), and the parties raise no question as to the appropriateness of the appeal.

2

RPD permits or applications are zoning permits, not building permits, and, as we later note, were an important part of the consent judgment which resulted from the lawsuit.

3

Paragraph 7 of the judgment modified the master plan to resolve the complaints raised in count IV, discussed above, and provided for concessions to both parties. For example, minimum lot size was increased to accommodate the city, but Pardee was accommodated to permit rezoning of parcels from park to commercial-recreational use.

4

Paragraph 6 reads in its entirety: "That by reason of the justified and good faith reliance of plaintiff as hereinabove set forth, plaintiff has a vested right to proceed with the development of all of the Property in the manner set out in Plaintiff's Master Plan as modified by this Judgment, and CITY, its agents, officers and employees, are estopped from adopting zoning or permanent land use regulation for the Property, which is in any manner inconsistent with Plaintiff's Master Plan and the zoning provided by Ordinance No. 178, except as herein expressly provided."

5

Paragraph 19 reads: "Nothing herein contained shall preclude CITY in the proper exercise of its police power from adopting any ordinance which will be applicable to PARDEE and the Property so long as such ordinance is not inconsistent with the provisions of this judgment which allows PARDEE to develop in accordance with the zoning and Master Plan submitted. It is the intent and purpose of this section that the CITY not be precluded from the exercise of its

136

broad police power relative to general subject matter which may be applicable to all builders and developers alike throughout the City. City, at any time after 15 years from the date hereof, may amend the zoning of the Property or any portion thereof in the proper exercise of the police power and if required in the public interest, safety, health, morals and general welfare. The CITY, upon determination that a zone change is need upon any portion of the Property and the failure of the parties to agree upon such zone change, may make application to the Court for modification of this Judgment to allow such rezoning upon proper showing of the need therefor."

6   The Growth Control Ordinance contained the following general provisions:

Section 20.04 set forth a declaration of purpose, stating that it was the intent of the people of the city to achieve a steady growth in order to properly provide new facilities and services, protect open space, and accomplish similar purposes.

The ordinance applied to all residential development and imposed a "Residential Development Control System" for the city, through December 31, 1995. The ordinance set a limit on the number of dwelling units which could be built in the entire city, per year, of 700 units in 1981 and 400 units in each year thereafter but authorized the city council to modify that number by 10 percent, more or less, in any year. (§ 20.07)

It exempted certain specified types of residential developments from its provisions (§ 20.05) and provided that no building permit for nonexempted projects could be issued until a development allotment for such project had been granted. (§ 20.08)

A "Residential Development Evaluation Board" would consider the applications for allotments. Each application would be examined for effects on water, fire, and other services; whether it had already received tentative tract map approval; and quality and environmental factors. (§ 20.09A) The development application would then be rated on a point system, and the evaluation board would hold a public hearing on the point assignments. The evaluation board would then report its evaluation and decisions to the city council (§ 20.09), which would then consider the recommendations and rankings at a public hearing and award allotments from among the number allowable for that year. (§ 20.10) If a developer did not receive a certain minimum number of points, he would be eliminated from

137

consideration. (§ 20.10) The city council was authorized to establish the maximum number of allotments that could be issued to a single developer in any one year.

7

Pardee has challenged the validity and constitutionality of the Growth Control Ordinance on its face and as applied in a separate action, pending in the Ventura County Superior Court. No such issue is raised in this proceeding.

8

Indeed, the master plan recited that the report and the included development plans "represent a request for zoning." The master plan therefore described the proposed development only in general terms; no specific, identifiable buildings were shown.

9

As a general rule, a developer must comply with the laws in effect at the time when a building permit is to be issued. (Hazon-Iny Development, Inc. v. City of Santa Monica (1982) 128 Cal.App.3d 1, 10-11 [179 Cal.Rptr. 860]) There is nothing in the judgment to indicate that the general rule was to be inapplicable. On the contrary, the judgment expressly provides that Pardee can obtain its tentative tract maps and other permits after "compliance with all legal requirements in order that the development of the Property may be completed in accordance with this Judgment." (Italics added)

10

The plaintiff does not challenge the constitutionality of the growth ordinance, except as applied. Thus I do not reach that profound issue in this proceeding.

11

The city relies on the rule that "a builder must comply with the laws which are in effect at the time a building permit is issued, including the laws which were enacted after application for the permit" (Avco, supra, 17 Cal.3d at p. 795) to claim that regardless of Pardee's vested right, it must comply with the ordinance whenever it seeks a building permit. But this reliance is misplaced. The judgment here acted as the equivalent of a building permit in order to create Pardee's vested right. Thus, the relevant law is that in existence at the time the judgment was entered, seven years before the ordinance was enacted.

Chapter 13

LEGAL CONSTRAINTS ON PUBLIC/PRIVATE NEGOTIATIONS: A CHECKLIST OF ISSUES AND CASES
Robert H. Freilich

In recent years, particularly in the antitrust and civil rights fields, litigation resulting from the development process has exploded in the federal courts. The statutory basis of such litigation is primarily twofold: the Sherman Antitrust Act and the Civil Rights Act of 1871. The following is an outline of the relevant cases, laws, and journal articles.

I. The Local Government Antitrust Act of 1984

The most important recent development concerning local governments' exposure to antitrust claims resulting from land use and other policies was adoption of the local Government Antitrust Act of 1984. (An important section of that act is included in an appendix.)

II. Municipal Liability under Antitrust Laws

A. Focus of the Sherman Act: Per se Analysis versus the Rule of Reason

1. Even though §1 of the Sherman Act prohibits "[e]very contract, combination...or conspiracy in restraint of trade," the Supreme Court has indicated that Congress intended only to outlaw <u>unreasonable</u> restraints of trade.

Standard Oil Co. v. United States, 221 U.S. 1 (1911).

Civiletti, The Fallout from Community Communications Co. v. City of Boulder: Prospects for a Legislative Solution, 32 Catholic L. Rev. 379 (1983).

2. Certain types of restraints are held to be unreasonable per se: "[T]here are certain agreements or practices which because of their pernicious effect on competition and lack of any redeeming virtue are conclusively presumed to be unreasonable and therefore illegal without elaborate inquiry as to the precise harm they have caused or the

business excuse for their use." <u>Northern Pacific Railroad Co.</u> v. <u>United States</u>, 356 U.S. 1 (1958).

<u>United States</u> v. <u>Socony-Vacuum Oil Co.</u>, 310 U.S. 150 (1940) (combinations formed for the purpose of price fixing are illegal per se).

3. If conduct is not illegal per se, the court will apply a <u>rule of reason</u> and therefore must inquire into the nature, purpose, and effect of the alleged restraint to determine its reasonableness and thus its legality.

    <u>Continental T.V., Inc.</u> v. <u>GTE Sylvania, Inc.</u>, 433 U.S. 36 (1977).

B. Relationship between the Police Power and the Rule of Reason

    1. If a local government is a defendant in an antitrust case, a "municipal rule of reason" or "public benefit defense" should apply.

    2. Balancing Test: Under the rule of reason, anticompetitive effects are balanced against possible procompetitive effects and other "public policy" factors. E.g., <u>Silver</u> v. <u>New York Stock Exchange</u>, 373 U.S. 341 (1963) (The exchange's need for regulation of its members outweighed the fact that some regulations had an anticompetitive effect.)

    3. If a municipality seeks to further the public health, safety, and welfare in a reasonable way (i.e., within the power), the contested action should survive a rule of reason analysis. See III, below.

    4. Where government is acting pursuant to legitimate police power goals, a per se analysis is never appropriate. Cf. <u>Affiliated Capital Corp.</u> v. <u>City of Houston</u>, 735 F.2d (5th Cir. 1984) (city's territorial division of cable TV market found to be illegal per se).

    5. The Sherman Act is "aimed <u>primarily</u> at combinations having <u>commercial objectives</u> and is <u>applied</u> to only a <u>very</u>

140

limited extent to organizations, like labor unions, <u>which</u>
<u>normally have other objectives</u>." <u>Klors, Inc.</u> v.
<u>Broadway-Hale Stores, Inc.</u>, 359 U.S. 207, 213 n. 7 (1959).

6. A decision by a municipal body that displaces competition
   in pursuit of some other public purpose seems to lack
   certain essential qualities of the type of conduct that
   normally falls under the ban of the Sherman Act.

   Vanderstar, <u>Liability of Municipalities under the</u>
   <u>Antitrust Laws: Litigation Strategies</u>, 32 Catholic
   University L. Rev. 395 (1983).

   <u>Kendrick</u> v. <u>City Council of Augusta</u>, 516 F. Supp. 1134
   (S.D. Ga. 1981) illustrates the difficulty courts may
   experience in finding the requisite effect on interstate
   commerce in local regulatory matters.

7. When governmental action comes within the scope of the
   police power, anticompetitive effects are not enough to
   find liability. Justice Brennan, in <u>Community</u>
   <u>Communications Co.</u> v. <u>City of Boulder</u>, noted that
   "anticompetitive effect is an insufficient basis for
   invalidating a state law." 455 U.S. 40, 56 (1982)

   See: <u>Exxon Corp.</u> v. <u>Governor of Maryland</u>, 437 U.S. 117,
   133 (1978) (anticompetitive effect alone not enough to
   establish liability, as state's power to regulate economic
   activity would be impaired)

C. The Proprietary/Governmental Distinction

1. Chief Justice Burger's concurring opinion in <u>City of</u>
   <u>Lafayette</u> v. <u>Louisiana Power & Light Co.</u>, 435 U.S. 389
   (1978) turned on this distinction. He apparently would
   hold local governments acting in a proprietary capacity to
   the same standard as any private commercial entity.

2. <u>Pueblo Aircraft Service, Inc.</u> v. <u>City of Pueblo</u>, 679 F.2nd
   805 (10th Cir. 1982), <u>cert.</u> <u>denied</u>, 459 U.S. 1126 (1983)
   (Tenth Circuit held that when legislature passed statute
   that authorized city to establish and maintain airports,

the fact that the legislature found that such would serve a public purpose transformed what would otherwise be a proprietary function into a governmental one.)

3. <u>Highfield Water Co.</u> v. <u>Public Service Commission</u>, 488 F. Supp. 1176 (D. Md. 1980) (Court adopted Burger's governmental/proprietary distinction and held that the <u>activity</u>, not the <u>identity</u>, of the party controls.)

D. <u>Noerr-Pennington</u> Immunity

1. This doctrine exempts from antitrust liability legitimate lobbying and other joint efforts by parties to influence legislative or executive action. See IV.B. below.

2. <u>Westborough Mall, Inc.</u> v. <u>City of Cape Girardeau</u>, 693 F.2d 733 (8th Cir. 1982), <u>cert. denied</u>, <u>Sub nom. Drury</u> v. <u>Westborough Mall Inc.</u>, 461 U.S. 945 (1983). (Plaintiffs argued that <u>Noerr-Pennington</u> should not apply because the city officials were alleged participants in the conspiracy.

(Court declined to base its refusal to exempt the defendants on the status of one of the participants, "[r]ather, we find that the defendants may not be protected by <u>Noerr</u> because their legitimate lobbying efforts may have been accompanied by illegal or fraudulent actions.... [T]the plaintiffs have presented facts that support an influence of unlawful conduct--City officials may have been induced by the May-Drury defendants by means other than legitimate lobbying to illegally revert plaintiff's C-4 zoning." <u>Id</u>. at 746.)

E. State Action Exemption

1. Citing <u>Community Communications</u> v. <u>City of Boulder</u>, 455 U.S. 40, 52 (1982), the court noted that "[t]he <u>Parker</u> doctrine applies to municipal action in furtherance or implementation of clearly articulated and affirmatively expressed state policy." <u>Westborough Mall</u>, 693 F.2d at 746.

142

2. "Even if zoning in general can be characterized as 'state action,'...a conspiracy to thwart normal zoning procedures and to directly injure the plaintiffs by illegally depriving them of their property is not in furtherance of any clearly articulated state policy." Id.

3. Thus, the state action exemption did not apply to any of the Westborough Mall defendants.

III. The "State Action" Exemption

A. Development of the Doctrine

1. Parker v. Brown, 317 U.S. 341 (1943) [The exercise of sovereign powers by a state is exempt from the proscriptions of the Sherman Act (case involved the validity of a California statute that sought to stabilize raising prices by authorizing limits on production).]

2. Goldfarb v. Virginia State Bar, 421 U.S. 773 (1975) involved a minimum attorneys' fee schedule published by the county bar and enforced by the Virginia state bar. The court held that the schedule was not exempt under Parker because the state agency's action was not "compelled by direction of the state act as sovereign." Id. at 791

3. Cantor v. Detroit Edison Co., 428 U.S. 579 (1976) (Even though Michigan Public Service Commission approved the utility's practice of distributing free light bulbs, the commission did not "compel" the practice and thus the court found no state action immunity.)

4. Bates v. State Bar of Arizona, 433 U.S. 350 (1977) (Disciplinary rule adopted by Arizona Supreme Court prohibiting advertising by attorneys was considered to be exempt state action because it was enforced and promulgated by "the ultimate body wielding the State's power over the practice of law" and therefore was "compelled by direction of the State acting as sovereign.") Id. at 360

5. <u>City of Lafayette</u> v. <u>Louisiana Power & Light Co.</u>, 435 U.S. 389 (1978) (When municipal utility competed with a private utility outside the city limits, the municipality did not enjoy state action immunity because the action taken was not "pursuant to state policy to displace competition with regulation or monopoly public service.") <u>Id.</u> at 413

B.   The <u>Midcal</u> Test

1. <u>California Retail Liquor Dealers Association</u> v. <u>Midcal Aluminum, Inc.</u>, 445 U.S. 97 (1980) established the following two-prong test to determine state action immunity: "First, the challenged restraint must be 'one clearly articulated and affirmatively expressed as state policy'; second, the policy must be 'actively supervised' by the state itself." <u>Id.</u> at 105 (quoting <u>City of Lafayette</u>, 435 U.S. at 410)

2. Areeda, <u>Antitrust Immunity for "State Action" after Lafayette</u>, 95 Harv. L. Rev. 435, 445 (1981) (Areeda suggests that the "active supervision" component should apply only to governmental supervision of <u>private</u> parties, as it was in <u>Midcal</u>.)

C.   <u>Boulder</u>

1. <u>Community Communications Co.</u> v. <u>City of Boulder</u>, 455 U.S. 40 (1982) involved a suit by the city's existing cable television franchisee, challenging an ordinance that prohibited new installations for three months, during which time other prospective franchisees were invited to bid.

2. The state's grant of <u>home rule</u> powers did not give rise to state action immunity because they are <u>neutral</u>. Passage of the ordinance was neither "the action of the State of Colorado itself in its sovereign capacity" nor "municipal action in furtherance of clearly articulated and affirmatively expressed state policy." <u>Id.</u> at 52

D.   "Clear Articulation and Affirmative Expression" in Land Use Cases

1.   Hybud Equipment Corp. v. City of Akron, 742 F.2d 949 (6th
     Cir. 1984) (Enabling legislation gave Ohio Water
     Development Authority power to deal with disposal of
     waste. The court found state action immunity because it
     was "unquestionable" that the legislature "contemplated
     the use of anticompetitive measures to ensure the
     financial viability of its waste disposal facilities."
     Id.

2.   Town of Hallie v. City of Eau Claire, _____ U.S.
     _____, 105 S.Ct.1713 (1985) (City's refusal to supply
     sewer treatment to neighboring towns that refused to be
     annexed was exempt from antitrust liability because
     enabling statutes gave city the authority to insist on
     annexation as a prerequisite to extending service. The
     state policy need not be compelled, only generally
     authorized, where a traditional municipal function is
     involved.)

3.   Pueblo Aircraft Service, Inc. v. City of Pueblo, 679 F.2d
     805 (10th Cir. 1982) (General statutory language
     authorizing the city to operate a municipal airport
     exempted the city from antitrust liability in dealing with
     its fixed base operators.)

4.   All American Cab Co. v. Metropolitan Knoxville Airport
     Authority, 547 F. Supp. 509 (E.D. Tenn. 1982), aff'd
     without opinion, 723 F.2d 908 (10th Cir. 1983)
     (Restraints on ground services at municipal airport found
     immune because operation of the airport benefited the
     general public, thus suggesting that regulations or
     actions furthering the public health, safety, or welfare
     should be exempt.)

5.   Highfield Water Co. v. Public Service Commission, 488 F.
     Supp. 1176 (D.Md. 1980) (Private utility brought suit in
     response to state takeover of its water system. The court
     found state action exemption, noting that local
     governments need not point to specific authorization but
     may rely on authority given in the general area and what
     was contemplated by the legislature.)

6. Schiessle v. Stephens, 525 F. Supp. 763, 776 (N.D. Ill. 1981) (No immunity here because statutes regarding redevelopment did not authorize, let alone compel, a municipality to "violate federal antitrust laws by passing a 'sham' redevelopment plan to further a conspiracy with private developers.")

7. Grason Electric Co. v. Sacramento Municipal Utility District, 526 F. Supp. 276 (E.D. Calif. 1981) (No immunity. City could not establish this "prong" of the Midcal test because "broad, general organic statutes" are not enough.)

8. Mason City Center Associates v. City of Mason City, 468 F. Supp. 737 (N.D. Iowa 1979), aff'd, 671 F.2d 1146 (8th Cir. 1982) (Shopping mall developer challenged city's zoning, which favored downtown shopping center instead. The court rejected the idea that grant of zoning power was sufficient authorization from the state.)

9. Westborough Mall, Inc. v. City of Cape Girardeau, 693 F.2d 733 (8th Cir. 1982) (Court reversed finding of immunity. Like Mason City, a finding of conspiracy led court to hold that even if grant of zoning power were sufficient state action, the exemption would not carry over to protect conspiracies that thwart or abuse the zoning process.)

10. Jonnet Development Corp. v. Caliguiri, 558 F. Supp. 962 (W.D. Pa. 1983) (Allegation that city conspired with private defendants to prevent plaintiff from acquiring property to construct hotel; state action exemption applicable where Pennsylvania's urban development statutes granted the city power to purchase property for redevelopment in blighted areas.)

11. Scott v. City of Sioux City, 1983-1 Trade Cas. (CCH) ¶65,352 (N.D. Iowa May 3, 1983) (Allegations of conspiracy to assure that regional shopping areas would not compete with downtown urban renewal efforts; state action exemption applicable where court found that displacement of competition in outlying areas was not unreasonable consequence of engaging in urban renewal.)

12. **Community Builders, Inc. v. City of Phoenix,** 652 F.2d 823 (9th Cir. 1981) (Plaintiff challenged water hookup fee where two cities had entered agreement that divided up water service in border areas; state action exemption applicable because state statute forbidding competition between municipal utilities authorized the displacement of competition with monopoly public service.)

13. **Shrader v. Horton,** 471 F. Supp. 1236 (W.D. Va. 1979), **aff'd on other grounds,** 626 F.2d 1163 (4th Cir. 1980) (Suit charging that mandatory water connection ordinance eliminated competition by private systems; state action exemption applicable where court found statute authorized such ordinances.)

E. "Active State Supervision" in Land Use Cases

1. **Town of Hallie v. City of Eau Claire,** _____ U.S. _____, 105 S.Ct. 1713 (1985) (Court held that where traditional government function is involved, **Midcal** does not require a finding of active supervision.)

2. **Hybud Equipment Corp. v. City of Akron,** 455 U.S. 931 (1982) held "active state supervision does **not** apply to municipalities engaged in a traditional municipal function."

3. Again Areeda, in **Antitrust Immunity for "State Action" after Lafayette,** 95 Harv. L. Rev. 435 (1981) argues that this prong applies only to supervision of **private** parties.

F. Summary: **Midcal** in the Land Use Context

1. Zoning is obviously a traditional municipal function under **Town of Hallie** and **Hybud,** and municipal defendants should thus (a) be able to rely on general enabling statutes to show "articulation and expression" and (b) for the same reason be able to dispense with the "active supervisory" requirement designed for private parties in **Midcal.**

2. Both **Hallie** and **Hybud** are consistent with **Boulder** because an **enabling** statute (even a broad one) has more

"authorization" than the general and <u>neutral</u> grant of home rule.

IV. Other Issues Affecting Municipal Antitrust Liability in the Land Use Context

A. Conspiracy

1. To establish liability under the Sherman Act, the plaintiff must prove the existence of a "contract, combination or conspiracy." §2

2. Although no decisions have been rendered regarding intraentity conspiracy among state agencies or conspiracy between public officials and state agencies, conspiracies between officials and private parties are prohibited under the Sherman Act.

   a. <u>Mason City Center Associates</u> v. <u>City of Mason City</u>, 468 F. Supp. 737 (N.D. Iowa 1979) (City could not rely on Iowa zoning statute to exempt it from antitrust liability where it was alleged that "zoning powers were exercised in furtherance of an unlawful anticompetitive agreement with private developers.")

   b. <u>Affiliated Capital Corp.</u> v. <u>City of Houston</u>, 735 F.2d 1555 (5th Cir. 1984) (Conspiracy found between city, public officials, and private party regarding award of CATV franchise.) See paragraph I(B)(4), <u>supra</u>.

   c. <u>Westborough Mall, Inc.</u> v. <u>City of Cape Girardeau</u>, 693 F.2d 733 (8th Cir. 1982) (Circumstantial evidence of an illegal agreement between private developer and city officials to stop or delay plaintiffs' shopping mall project was sufficient to preclude summary judgment for defendants on a conspiracy count.)

   d. <u>Cedar-Riverside Associates, Inc.</u> v. <u>United States</u>, 459 F. Supp. 1290 (D. Minn. 1978), <u>aff'd</u>, 606 F.2d 254 (8th Cir. 1979) (State action exemption would normally be available to municipal activities under state's redevelopment act; however, complaint alleged conspiracy between municipal defendants and a private party to restrain competition and exclude participation in plaintiff developer's urban renewal project, and therefore the claims could not be dismissed on grounds of immunity.)

e. Stauffer v. Town of Grand Lake, 1981-1 Trade Cas. (CCH) ¶64,029 (D. Colo. Oct. 9, 1980) (Although Colorado zoning enabling legislation clearly showed a state policy that some competition would be displaced by regulation, state action immunity was inapplicable where plaintiff alleged that town's downzoning of plaintiff's property was result of conspiracy motivated by personal gain for town officials.)

f. Nelson v. Utah County, 1978-1 Trade Cas. (CCH ¶62,128 (D. Utah 1977) (No state action immunity for rezoning ordinance preventing full economic use of plaintiff's property where plaintiff alleged local official benefited thereby.)

3. A lawfully enacted zoning ordinance can constitute part of a conspiracy to exclude retail liquor business. See Whitworth v. Perkins, 559 F.2d 378 (5th Cir. 1977), vacated and remanded sub nom., City of Impact v. Whitworth, 435 U.S. 992, reinstated on remand, 576 F.2d 696 (5th Cir. 1978), cert. denied, 440 U.S. 911 (1979).

4. Cooperation agreements: Unity Ventures v. County of Lake (N.D. Ill. 1984), Case No. 81 C 2745.

B. Noerr-Pennington

1. The Basic Doctrine

a. "[T]he Sherman Act does not apply to the activities...compris[ing] mere solicitation of governmental action with respect to the passage and enforcement of laws."

"[We hold] that, at least insofar as the railroad's campaign was directed towards obtaining governmental

149

action, its legality was not at all affected by any anticompetitive purpose it may have had."

Eastern Railroad Presidents Conference v. Noerr Motor Freight, Inc., 356 U.S. 127, 138-40 (1961) (doctrine based on the protection of the First Amendment).

b. "Joint efforts to influence public officials do not violate the antitrust laws even though intended to eliminate competition. Such conduct is not illegal, either standing alone or as part of a broader scheme itself violative of the Sherman Act."

UMW v. Pennington, 381 U.S. 657, 670 (1965).

c. Noerr and Pennington, which involved the legislative and executive branches, have been extended to the judicial branch and administrative agencies.

California Motor Transport Co. v. Trucking Unlimited, 404 U.S. 508, 510-11 (1972).

2. The "Sham" Exception to Noerr-Pennington

a. The immunity afforded to defendants when they are attempting to influence the legislative process is not unlimited. Such attempts will be actionable where they are "a mere sham to cover what is actually nothing more than an attempt to interfere directly with the business relationships of a competitor...."

Noerr, 365 U.S. at 144.

b. The "sham" exception was extended in California Motor Transport to situations involving "unethical conduct in the setting of the adjudicatory process" or the pursuit of "a pattern of baseless, repetitive claims." These practices cannot be protected by Noerr-Pennington because they are an abuse of process and effectively bar access.

150

c. The practices of the owners of established shopping
    centers attempting to prevent plaintiffs from opening
    a competing shopping center fell within the "sham"
    exception:

>   [B]y the bringing of numerous meritless appeals,
>   by deliberate delay in the prosecution of those
>   appeals, by the solicitation and subsidization
>   of meritless litigation by landowners, and by
>   their attorney's failure to convey a settlement
>   offer,...the defendants successfully stalled
>   plaintiffs' applications for zoning changes on
>   the Evergreen Avenue property for five years.
>   This delay ultimately forced the plaintiffs to
>   abandon their venture. We hold that these
>   allegations state a cause of action under the
>   antitrust laws.

>   Landmarks Holding Corp. v. Bermant, 664 F.2d
>   891, 896 (2d Cir. 1981)

d. A litigant claiming the "sham" exception must state
    his allegations "in more than conclusory terms; his
    complaint must provide some basis for believing what
    appears to be an exercise of the right to petition is
    in reality something else."

>   City of Newark v. Delmarva Power & Light Co., 497 F.
>   Supp. 323, 326 (D. Del. 1980) (Defendant failed to
>   make any specific allegations that city raised "sham"
>   issues at Federal Power Commission hearings to delay
>   proceedings and force plaintiffs into unfair
>   settlements.)

>   But cf. Mason City Center Associates v. City of Mason
>   City, 468 F. Supp. 737 (N.D. Iowa 1979) (Plaintiff's
>   complaint alleging that city entered agreement with
>   private developers to prevent construction of a
>   competing shopping center and that developers
>   deprived plaintiffs of meaningful access to city's
>   zoning mechanisms did not fail to state a cause of
>   action; facts determining whether Noerr-Pennington

151

applied were in the hands of the alleged
co-conspirator.)

    e.   City's mere belief that intervention would delay the
proceedings is not sufficient to establish "sham"
conduct. Newark, 497 F. Supp. at 327

    f.   Given its constitutional basis, the Noerr-Pennington
doctrine will shield a defendant from claims based on
state common law claims as well. Id. at 328

3.   Noerr-Pennington does not protect fraudulent or illegal
actions to influence a legislative decision. Westborough
Mall v. City of Cape Girardeau, 693 F.2d 733, 746 (8th
Cir. 1982)

4.   Noerr-Pennington should not apply in cases where
governmental officials are alleged participants in the
conspiracy.

See Duke & Co. v. Forester, 521 F.2d 1277, 1282 (3d Cir.
1975) (Noerr held inapplicable where "governmental
participation" in combination and public body's actions
"not compelled by state.")

Affiliated Capital Corp. v. City of Houston, 735 F.2d 1555
(5th Cir. 1984) (Noerr would protect joint efforts to
persuade public officials "unless one or more of the
public officials involved was also a participant in an
illegal arrangement or conspiracy.") See also paragraph
I(B)(4), supra.

But see Metro Cable Co. v. CATV of Rockford, Inc., 516
F.2d 220 (7th Cir. 1975) (Co-conspirator exception
criticized); Westborough Mall v. City of Cape Girardeau,
693 F.2d 733 (8th Cir. 1982)

See also:

Miracle Mile Associates v. City of Rochester, 617 F.2d 18
(2d Cir. 1980) (City actively opposed shopping center in
suburb that would be in competition with proposed downtown

shopping center and filed administrative proceedings to force suburban developer to comply with state and federal environmental regulations; city's actions exempt under Noerr-Pennington doctrine.)

C. Treble Damage Liability for Municipalities for Anticompetitive Acts

1. City of Newport v. Fact Concerts, Inc., 453 U.S. 247 (1981) (Punitive damages not available from municipalities in §1983 suits.)

2. Rehnquist's dissent in Boulder suggests that it could be difficult to maneuver around the "mandatory" language of §4 of the Clayton Act. This view was also adopted by the district court in Grason Electric Co. v. Sacramento Municipal Utility District, 526 F. Supp. 276 (E.D. Calif. 1981).

3. Grason held that Fact Concerts is distinguishable from antitrust cases because §1983 was intended to incorporate common law immunities, while §4 of the Clayton Act clearly mandates the payment of treble damages.

4. Richmond Hilton Associates v. City of Richmond, 690 F.2d 1086 (4th Cir. 1982) (Fourth Circuit, in dicta, assumed that treble damages would be available from a municipality.)

V. Summary of Recent Developments Magnifying the Importance of Section 1983

Section 1 of The Civil Rights Act of 1871, codified as amended at 42 U.S.C. Section 1983 (1982):

Twenty percent of the current civil case load in federal courts is litigation invoking Section 1983 of the Civil Rights Act of 1871. Typically, plaintiffs are seeking to top the "deep pocket" of public treasuries for claimed damages. The text of Section 1983 follows:

§ 1983. Civil action for deprivation of rights

Every person who, under color of any statute, ordinance, regulation, custom or usage, of any State or Territory or the District of Columbia, subjects, or causes to be subjected, any citizen of the United States or other person within the jurisdiction thereof to the deprivation of any rights, privileges, or immunities secured by the Constitution and laws, shall be liable to the party injured in an action at law, suit in equity, or other proper proceeding for redress. For the purposes of this section, any Act of Congress applicable exclusively to the District of Columbia shall be considered to be a statute of the District of Columbia.

A. The Civil Rights Attorney's Fees Awards Act of 1976, 42 U.S.C. § 1988, plus Hensley v. Eckerhart, 461 U.S. 424 (1983) (extent of success measures amount of attorney's fee award)

B. Expansion of local entity liability: Monell v. Department of Social Services, 436 U.S. 658 (1978); Owen v. City of Independence, 445 U.S. 622 (1980) (no entity immunity from statutory liability). Owen itself, 623 F.2d 550 (8th Cir. 1980) (on remand from 445 U.S. 622), and cases like Supreme Court of Virginia v. Consumers Union, 446 U.S. 719 (1980) leave question open as to immunity from general and special damages (sounding in tort) -- distinguish between immunity from liability and immunity (and other defenses) to particular remedies. See also, Facts Concerts (immunity from punitive damages) and Monell (immunity for respondeat superior liability).

C. Definition of state entity immunity under the 11th Amendment: Edelman v. Jordan, 415 U.S. 651 (1974); Fitzpatrick v. Bitzer, 427 U.S. 445 (1976).

D. Application of Section 1983 as a vehicle to litigate federal statutory claims: Maine v. Thiboutot, 448 U.S. 1 (1980); Federal Question Jurisdiction Amendment Act of 1980 [limited by Middlesex County Sewerage Authority v. National Sea Clammers Association, 453 U.S. 1 (1981)].

E. Expansion of individual officer liability exposure under the good faith immunity defense (encompassing an objective standard): Wood v. Strickland, 420 U.S. 308 (1975); Wood standard narrowed by Harlow v. Fitzgerald, 457 U.S. 800 (1982) [A Bivens case relevant to § 1983 by analogy that took the subjective "good faith" test out of the qualified immunity defense. Question remains as to degree of culpability necessary as part of plaintiff's prima facie case to get damages sounding in tort. Adickes v. S.H. Kress & Co., 398 U.S. 144 (1970).] State legislators and judges exercising a state's entire legislative authority over a subject are absolutely immune from all actions (damages, declaratory, and injunctive relief), but prosecutors are protected only against damage suits [Supreme Court of Virginia v. Consumers Union, 446 U.S. 719 (1980)]

F. "State action" equated to "under color of state law": Lugar v. Edmondson Oil Co., 457 U.S. 922 (1982), rev'g 639 F.2d 1058 (4th Cir. 1981).

G. A public defender does not always act under color of state law: Polk County v. Dodson, 454 U.S. 312 (1981), rev'g 628 F.2d 1104 (8th Cir. 1980).

H. No exhaustion of administrative remedies: Patsy v. Florida Board of Regents, 457 U.S. 496 (1982), rev'g 634 F.2d 900 (5th Cir. 1981) (en banc).

I. Abstention (Young v. Kenley, 641 F.2d 192 (4th Cir. 1981), cert. denied, sub nom. Long v. Bonnes, 455 U.S. 961 (1982) for state bar disciplinary proceedings.

J. Smith v. Wade, 461 U.S. 30 (1983): punitive damages allowed without malicious intent.

K. Parratt v. Taylor, 451 U.S. 527 (1981): procedural due process and the arguable expansion to include "negligence" in certain cases. Block, Tower, Smith, and the plaintiff's prima facie case.

VI. Remedies

A. Damages

Sullivan v. Little Hunting Park, Inc., 396 U.S. 229 (1969):

"Compensatory damages for deprivation of a federal right are
governed by federal standards as provided by Congress in 42
U.S.C. § 1988....Both federal and state rules on damages may be
utilized, whichever better serves the policies expressed in the
federal statutes....The rule of damages, whether drawn from
federal or state sources, is a federal rule responsive to the
need, whenever a federal right is impaired." Federal policies
can always overcome any state rule of law--whether regarding
immunity, limitations, damages, etc.--and is what gives § 1983
litigation its special flavor and makes it a "field of evolving
definition and uncertainty" [Fact Concerts, 453 U.S. 247
(1981)].

1. Section 1983 reflects a congressional judgment that a
   "damages remedy against the offending party is a vital
   component of any scheme for indicating cherished
   constitutional guarantees." Owen v. City of Independence,
   445 U.S. 622 (1980); Gomez v. Toledo, 446 U.S. 635 (1980)

2. Carey v. Piphus, 435 U.S. 247 (1978), held that the
   cardinal principal of damages under Section 1983 is
   compensation for the injury caused; that there is no
   presumption of compensable injury even though the
   defendant's breach of duty is of constitutional dimension;
   that the plaintiff must prove damages caused by
   defendant's breach; and that emotional or mental distress
   can be included in a Section 1983 damages judgment if
   proven.

3. Carey v. Piphus, supra, held that nominal damages not to
   exceed one dollar should be awarded when a constitutional
   violation has been established but no actual injury is
   proved; such an award would appear to be sufficient to
   allow a court to award the plaintiff attorneys' fees under
   the Civil Rights Attorney's Fees Awards Act of 1976.

4. <u>Carey</u> v. <u>Piphus</u>, <u>supra</u>, left open the question of whether a punitive damages award would ever be appropriate in Section 1983 cases for the purpose of deterring or punishing violation of constitutional rights. n. 11. Further guidance on this issue comes from <u>Smith</u> v. <u>Wade</u>, 461 U.S. 30 (1983) (malicious intent not necessary for punitive damages; reckless or callous disregard sufficient).

B. Injunctions

The Supreme Court's primary focus on Section 1983 has been on monetary liability under Section 1983, with emphasis on damages and attorneys' fees. It would be shortsighted, however, to overlook the fiscal implications that can attach to equitable relief under Section 1983. First, plaintiffs who obtain injunctive relief under Section 1983 are entitled to an award of attorneys' fees under Section 1988. Second, governmental compliance with injunctions frequently can be expensive, particularly structural injunctions and injunctions affecting social benefit programs.

1. Declaratory and/or injunctive relief is generally available when a violation of constitutional rights has been found. Such relief is available even though no monetary recovery may be possible because of the good faith or absolute immunity of the official committing the constitutional violation, or because the governmental employee is employed by the state. <u>Monell</u>, 436 U.S. 658 (1978)

    a. <u>Monell</u> was a suit in equity.

    b. <u>Monell</u> established the "official policy" test for <u>municipal</u> liability (as opposed to <u>individual</u> liability).

    c. Municipal liability--even for injunctive or declaratory relief--then would require:

        1) "official paper" (ordinance, charter, resolution, etc.)

157

2) custom

3) acts by those who may fairly be said to represent official policy or

4) failure to supervise [under Rizzo v. Goode, 423 U.S. 362 (1976)--where the test was established, but Rehnquist found the mayor, city manager, and police commissioner not liable].

2. The structural injunction has been subjected to rigorous standing and chain of command requirements [O'Shea v. Littleton, 414 U.S. 488 (1974) and Rizzo v. Goode, 423 U.S. 362 (1976)], and the principle that the scope of the remedy must correlate with the extent of the constitutional violation [Dayton Board of Education v. Brinkman, 433 U.S. 406 (1977), reh'g denied, 444 U.S. 887 (1979).

   a. Further guidance came when the Court decided City of Los Angeles v. Lyons, 461 U.S. 95 (1983) (5 to 4 decision) in which an injunction against the use of chokeholds by the Los Angeles Police Department was held to be an improper interference with local police procedures.

      Plaintiff lacked standing because (a) he suffered a past wrong; (b) no likelihood that he would suffer wrong in the future, i.e., no basis for injunction, (c) adequacy of damage remedy; (d) avoiding third party rights in the future.

   b. A notable exception to this trend has been the employment discrimination area. Most of these cases arise under Title VII, but they can be litigated under Section 1983 when a constitutional violation is alleged. In addition to back pay and injunctive relief prohibiting unlawful practices or hiring criteria, courts have fashioned remedies requiring affirmative recruitment and hiring (including interim quotas) and awards of retroactive seniority to discriminatees. See Carter v. Gallagher, 452 F.2d

158

315 (8th Cir.) (en banc), cert. denied, 406 U.S. 950 (1972). The Court has granted cert. in Boston Chapter Firefighters Union v. Boston NAACP, Inc., No. 103 S.Ct. 3561 (1983), to decide whether a court can override seniority rights of white firefighters to preserve the level of integration achieved pursuant to an affirmative hiring order issued by the court after a finding of class-based discrimination.

3. An injunction issued by federal court in a Section 1983 case is not barred by the Anti-Injunction Act, 28 U.S.C § 2283, from staying state court proceedings, because Section 1983 has been found to come within the "expressly authorized by Act of Congress" exception to that statute. Mitchum v. Foster, 407 U.S. 225 (1972). Other "principles of equity, comity, and federalism," however, have proven to impose considerable restraints on federal courts when asked to enjoin state proceedings in 1983 suits. See Younger v. Harris, 401 U.S. 37 (1971) and progeny. But see Fair Assessment in Real Estate Association v. McNary, 454 U.S. 100 (1981) (St. Louis) (State taxpayers are barred from asserting tax claims under § 1983 under comity and Tax Injunction Act, 28 U.S.C. § 1341.)

C. Attorneys' Fees

1. The American Rule: Alyeska Pipeline Service Co. v. Wilderness Society, 421 U.S. 240 (1975), holding that fees could not be awarded by federal courts under the private attorney general theory in the absence of statutory authorization.

2. The Civil Rights Attorney's Fees Awards Act of 1976, 42 U.S.C. § 1988, expressly authorized a fees award to the prevailing party in "any action or proceeding to enforce" Section 1983. Hensley v. Eckerhart, 461 U.S. 424 (1983): the "extent of a plaintiff's success is a crucial factor in determining the proper amount"; unsuccessful claims distinct from successful claims should be excluded and where limited success has been achieved, fees should be reasonable in relation to that success.

3. Section 1988 has been construed to provide a dual standard, enabling prevailing civil plaintiffs virtually automatic recovery of fees, while restricting prevailing defendants' recovery of fees to frivolous or bad faith claims. Supreme Court of Virginia v. Consumers Union, 446 U.S. 719 n. 17 (1980), implicitly approves the attorneys' fees standard of Newman v. Piggie Park Enterprises, 390 U.S. 400, 402 (1968), that a prevailing plaintiff should ordinarily be awarded fees "unless special circumstances would render such an award unjust." In Christiansburg Garment Co. v. EEOC, 434 U.S. 412, 422 (1978), a Title VII case, the Court held that fees could be awarded to a prevailing defendant where a court finds that plaintiff's lawsuit "was frivolous, unreasonable, or groundless, or that the plaintiff continued to litigate after it clearly became so." See Huges v. Rowe, 449 U.S. 5, 14-15 (1980). But in a Title VII discrimination case, the 8th Circuit reversed a district court's award of defendant's attorneys' fees because plaintiff's claims were not frivolous or malicious. Bowers v. Kraft Foods Corp., 606 F.2d 816 (8th Cir. 1979).

4. The legislative history of Section 1988 recognizes the complexity of most civil rights litigation and its contingent nature and states that awards of fees to plaintiffs should be similar to those awarded in antitrust litigation. S. Rep. No. 94-1011, 94th Congress, 2d Session, 6 (1976). See Larson, Attorneys' Fees under the Civil Rights Attorneys' Fees Awards Act of 1976, 15 Clearinghouse Rev. 309, 317 (1981). See also Rajender v. University of Minnesota, 546 F. Supp. 158 (D.Minn. 1982) (fees award of $1.95 million in Title VII civil rights case).

5. Maher v. Gagne, 448 U.S. 122 (1980), holds that a plaintiff is entitled to fee award as the "prevailing party" even though the case was settled by consent decree without a judicial determination of liability.

6. Maine v. Thiboutot, 448 U.S. 1 (1980), holds that fee awards can be made under Section 1988 even when the case is brought in state court.

7. White v. New Hampshire Department of Employment Security,
    455 U.S. 445 (1982), holds that a postjudgment request for
    fees under Section 1988 is not subject to the 10-day time
    limit of Rule 59(e); the Court noted that district courts
    remain free to adopt local rules establishing time limits
    for fee requests. See Local Rule 2.9 for S. and N.D.
    Iowa, which provides that all postjudgment motions for
    award of attorneys' fees shall be filed within 20 days of
    entry of judgment (unless a statute provides a' longer
    time).

8. Blum v. Stenson, _____ U.S. _____, 104 S.Ct. 1541
    (1984), holds that there may be situations where the basic
    standard of reasonable attorneys' fees is unreasonably
    low. "[I]n some cases of exceptional success an enhanced
    award may be justified....The burden of providing that
    such an adjustment is necessary to the determination of a
    reasonable fee is on the fee applicant." Id. at 1548

VII. The Elements of the Section 1983 Cause of Action

See generally Mahoney, The Prima Facie Section 1983 Case, 14 Urban
Lawyer 131 (1982). Gomez v. Toledo, 446 U.S. 635, 640 (1980).

By the plain terms of § 1983, two--and only two--allegations
are required in order to state a cause of action under that
statute [i.e., for statutory liability]. First, the plaintiff
must allege that some person has deprived him of a federal
right. Second, he must allege that the person who has deprived
him of that right has acted under color of state or territorial
law.

A. Every person who... [who may be defendant]

1. Monell v. Department of Social Services, 436 U.S. 658
    (1978), holds that cities are "persons" within the meaning
    of Section 1983 and can be subjected to statutory
    liability; Monell also holds that cities cannot be found
    liable on a respondeat superior theory.

2. States are apparently "persons" within the meaning of
    Section 1983 too, but they can raise the 11th Amendment as

a bar to suit in federal court; however, the states can be sued under Section 1983 in state court, and Maine v. Thiboutot, 448 U.S. 1 (1980) and the 11th Amendment may not apply.

B. Under color of any statute...

1. Polk County v. Dodson, 454 U.S. 312 (1981), holds that a full-time public defender employed by the county does not act "under color of state law" when performing a lawyer's traditional functions as counsel to an indigent defendant in a state criminal proceeding. The defender's exercise of independent professional judgment in the proceeding in which she is the adversary of the state distinguishes the case from Branti v. Finkel, 445 U.S. 507 (1980), which found that a public defender's action in making hiring and firing decisions did constitute action under color of state law. Lugar v. Edmondson Oil Co., 457 U.S. 922 (1982), challenged conduct constituting state action is also under color of state law (state ex parte attachment statute); Blum v. Yaretsky, 457 U.S. 991 (1982), discharges from nursing homes not state action or state function; Lake County Estates, Inc. v. Lake Tahoe Regional Planning Agency, 440 U.S. 391 (1979), requirement of federal approval of an interstate compact did not foreclose a finding that the planning agency's conduct was "under color of state law."

2. The complex problem of when private conduct will be considered "state action" for purposes of suit under Section 1983 is beyond the scope of this chapter. The Supreme Court continues the trend toward restricting the attribution of such conduct to the state [Rendell-Baker v. Kohn, 457 U.S. 830 (1982); Blum v. Yaretsky, 457 U.S. 991 (1982); Lugar v. Edmondson Oil Co., 457 U.S. 922 (1982)]

C. Subjects, or causes to be subjected...

1. Monell v. Department of Social Services, supra, held that municipalities cannot be subjected to liability under respondeat superior. Monell held that a municipality

162

could be held liable under Section 1983 when "the action that is alleged to be unconstitutional implements or executes a policy statement, ordinance, regulation, or decision officially adopted and promulgated by that body's officers." 436 U.S. at 690. Monell further held that local governments could be sued for constitutional violations visited pursuant to governmental "custom." Id. Some circuits (e.g., the 5th) have added a third test: municipal liability for those acting as the final repository of authority. Compare Bennett v. City of Slidell, 735 F.2d 861 (5th Cir. 1984) to Familias Unidas v. Briscoe, 619 F.2d 391 (5th Cir. 1980). Also, Rizzo v. Goode, 423 U.S. 362 (1976) may have added a fourth test: failure to supervise.

2. Polk County v. Dodson, supra, characterizes Monell as holding that official policy must be "the moving force of the constitutional violation" (emphasis added) to establish the liability of government body under § 1983. Dodson ordered dismissed the claims against Polk County, the offender advocate, and the Board of Supervisors based on bald allegations that the defender had injured Dodson while acting pursuant to administrative "rules and procedures for..." handling criminal appeals and that the county "retains and maintains, advocates out of law school" who have on numerous occasions moved to withdraw from appeals of convictions. Court suggests that general allegations of administrative negligence do not state a Section 1983 claim against entities.

3. Martinez v. California, 444 U.S. 277, 285 (1980), finds that the actions of the parolee (in murdering the plaintiff's daughter five months after release on parole) were too remote from the time of release or "too remote a consequence of the parole officers' action to hold them responsible" under Section 1983.

4. Mt. Healthy City School District Board of Education v. Doyle, 429 U.S. 274 (1977), holds that where the plaintiff has made out a prima facie 1983 case by demonstrating that a constitutionally impermissible factor was a cause of plaintiff's injury, the burden of proof shifts to the

defendant to prove that it would have reached the same decision or result had it acted in compliance with plaintiff's constitutional rights (i.e., "valid considerations...motivated its actions").

D. Any citizens or other person... [who may be plaintiff]

1. Plyer v. Doe, 457 U.S. 202 (1982), held that undocumented alien children were "persons" within the meaning of both the due process and equal protection clauses of the 14th Amendment and implicitly within the meaning of Section 1983.

2. Whether an injured party's survivors can bring suit under Section 1983 turns on the law of the state in which the district court is sitting, as long as that law is not "inconsistent with the Constitution and laws of the United States," 42 U.S.C. § 1988. Robertson v. Wegmann, 436 U.S. 584 (1978), requires the dismissal of a 1983 action where the plaintiff died after the action was commenced and there were no relatives who could have maintained a survivor's action under state law.

E. To the deprivation of any rights...secured by the Constitution and Laws....

1. Maine v. Thiboutot, 448 U.S. 1 (1980), holds that Section 1983 encompasses claims based on purely statutory violations of federal law, such as the plaintiffs' claim that the state welfare department had deprived them of welfare benefits to which they were entitled under the federal Social Security Act. The Thiboutot dissent argued that Section 1983 provided a cause of action only for violations of federal statutes providing for the equal rights of citizens.

2. Pennhurst State School & Hosp. v. Helderman, 451 U.S. 1, 28 (1981), suggests an exception to Thiboutot whenever the violation alleged is not "'a right secured' by the laws of the United States within the meaning of Section 1983," or whenever the legislative remedy is exclusive.

3. <u>Middlesex County Sewage Authority</u> v. <u>National Sea Clammers Association</u>, 453 U.S. 1, 19 (1981), confirmed that there are two exceptions to the application of Section 1983 to statutory violations: "(i) whether Congress has foreclosed private enforcement of that statute in the enactment itself, and (ii) whether the statute at issue there was the kind that created enforceable 'rights' under Section 1983." When the federal statute provides its own remedial scheme, <u>National Sea Clammers</u> effectively places the burden on the 1983 plaintiff to show that Congress intended to extend Section 1983 remedies to cover the federally created statutory rights. <u>See</u> <u>The Supreme Court Term</u>, 95 Harv. L. Rev. 290, 298-299 (1981).

VIII. Section 1983 Defenses

<u>See</u> generally Rushing & Bratcher, <u>Section 1983 Defenses</u>, 14 The Urban Lawyer 149 (1982).

A.   Individual Immunity

1.   Absolute Individual Immunity

Absolute individual immunity is primarily enjoyed by judges, legislators, and prosecutors, and by other officials acting in a judicial, quasi-judicial, legislative, or quasi-legislative capacity. Recent case law suggests that such immunity depends upon the function of the duties performed by the official and not necessarily upon the official's job title. <u>See</u> <u>Supreme Court of Virginia</u> v. <u>Consumers Union</u>, 446 U.S. 719 (1980).

a.   Legislative Immunity (<u>Not</u> 11th)

(1)   Legislative immunity of state legislator bars not only suits for damages but also suits for declaratory judgment or injunctive relief; <u>see</u> <u>Supreme Court of Virginia</u> v. <u>Consumers Union</u>, 446 U.S. at 732.

(2)   Court distinguishes the legislative role of the Virginia Supreme Court from the rulemaking

authority commonly exercised by executive and agency officials because the Virginia Court claimed "inherent power to regulate the bar" and "the Virginia Court is exercising the State's entire legislative power with respect to regulating the bar and its members are the State's legislators for the purpose of issuing the Bar Code." Supreme Court of Virginia v. Consumers Union, 446 U.S. at 731. The Court makes clear that Section 1983 injunctive suit to prevent state officers from enforcing an unconstitutional law would still be appropriate. 446 U.S. at 736

(3) Lake Country Estates, Inc. v. Tahoe Regional Planning Agency, supra, left open the question of whether individuals performing legislative functions at the "purely local level" should also be afforded absolute legislative immunity. 440 U.S. at 404 n. 26

b. Judicial Immunity

(1) Judicial immunity protects state judges from damages liability for acts performed in their judicial capacities, but the Court has never held that it absolutely insulates judges from declaratory or injunctive relief. Supreme Court of Virginia v. Consumers Union, 446 U.S. at 735. Although the Court did not decide this issue in Consumers Union, it noted that the many courts of appeals that had addressed the issue concluded that judicial immunity did not extend to declaratory or injunctive relief. 446 U.S. at 735 n. 13

(2) State officials with enforcement authority, even those that are immune from damages liability, such as judges and prosecutors, can still be sued for injunctive relief under Section 1983 when they are threatening to enforce or are

enforcing an allegedly unconstitutional law. Consumer Union, 446 U.S. at 736

c. Officials Afforded Absolute Immunity

(1) Judge acting in a judicial capacity--Stump v. Sparkman, 435 U.S. 349 (1978)

(2) Administrative hearing examiners and others with adjudicatory responsibility--Butz v. Economou, 438 U.S. 478 (1978)

(3) Judge acting in rulemaking capacity in formulating ethics code is entitled to absolute legislative immunity but only to good faith immunity when judge is acting in enforcement capacity as to those rules--Supreme Court of Virginia v. Consumers Union, supra.

(4) Legislator acting in a legislative capacity-- Tenney v. Brandhove, 341 U.S. 367 (1951)

(5) Planning agency comprised of nonelected board acting in a legislative capacity--Lake Country Estates, Inc. v. Tahoe Regional Planning Agency, 440 U.S. 391 (1979)

(6) Prosecutor acting in prosecutorial capacity-- Imbler v. Pachtman, 424 U.S. 409 (1976)

(7) Administrative agency staff attorneys acting in prosecutorial capacity in agency contested case--Butz v. Economou, supra

(8) The president when acting within the "outer perimeter" of the duties of office--Nixon v. Fitzgerald, 457 U.S. 731 (1982)

(9) High-level executive officials, whether Cabinet or White House presidential aides, only when one can "show that the responsibilities of his office embraced a function so sensitive as to

require a total shield from liability" and "that he was discharging the protected function when performing the act for which liability is asserted." Harlow v. Fitzgerald, 457 U.S. 800, 813 (1982); see also Butz v. Economou, supra.

(10) Derivative immunity has been rejected when asserted by Cabinet officers and presidential aides, Butz and Fitzgerald, and by individuals conspiring with a judge, Dennis v. Sparks, 449 U.S. 24 (1980).

2. Qualified or Good Faith Immunity

   a. Public officials who are not afforded absolute immunity are entitled to assert an affirmative defense of "qualified" immunity. Gomez v. Toledo, 446 U.S. at 640. The Court has not decided the question of which party bears the burden of proof on the issue of qualified immunity. Harlow v. Fitzgerald, 457 U.S. at 815 n. 24. Burden of pleading is on defendant. Gomez.

   b. A subjective-objective standard for this defense was first developed in Wood v. Strickland, 420 U.S. 308 (1975), in the context of disciplinary action taken by a school board, and the Wood standard has subsequently been quoted as the general statement of the qualified immunity standard. Qualified immunity would be defeated if an official "knew or reasonably should have known that the action he took within his sphere of official responsibility would violate the constitutional rights of the [plaintiff], or if he took the action with malicious intention to cause a deprivation of constitutional rights or other injury...." Id. at 321-22

   c. The Supreme Court repudiated the subjective aspect of the Wood standard in a constitutional suit against the federal officials, a ruling

that the Court indicated would also apply in
Section 1983 actions against state officials.
Harlow v. Fitzgerald, 457 U.S. at 818 n. 30.
Concluding that "substantial costs attend the
litigation of the subjective good faith of
government officials," Harlow v. Fitzgerald
held "that governmental officials performing
discretionary functions generally are shielded
from liability for civil damages insofor as
their conduct does not violate clearly
established statutory or constitutional rights
of which a reasonable person would have known."
457 U.S. at 818

d.   Officials Afforded Good Faith Immunity

    (1) Pierson v. Ray, 386 U.S. 547 (1967) (police
         officer)

    (2) Scheuer v. Rhodes, 416 U.S. 232 (1974)
         (governor)

    (3) O'Connor v. Donaldson, 422 U.S. 563 (1975)
         (state hospital administrator)

    (4) Wood v. Strickland, supra (school board
         members)

    (5) Procunier v. Navarette, 434 U.S. 555 (1978)
         (prison officials)

e.   Youngberg v. Romeo, 457 U.S. 307 (1982), where
      in the context of hospital professionals, the
      Court stated that good faith immunity would bar
      liability if the professional "was unable to
      satisfy his normal professional standards
      because of budgetary constraints."

B. Entity Liability

    1. Local Governmental Entities

        a. Local governmental bodies can be sued directly under Section 1983 "for monetary, declaratory, or injunctive relief where the action that is alleged to be unconstitutional implements or executes a policy statement, ordinance, regulation, or decision officially adopted and promulgated by that body's officers." Monell v. Department of Social Services, 436 U.S. at 690. Furthermore, local governments "may be sued for constitutional deprivations visited pursuant to governmental 'custom' even though such a custom has not received formal approval through the body's official decisionmaking channels." Id.

        b. A municipality cannot be held liable, however, solely because it employs a tortfeasor; a municipality cannot be held liable under Section 1983 on a respondeat superior theory. Monell, 436 U.S. at 691

        c. Municipalities cannot assert qualified immunity as a defense to statutory liability. Owen v. City of Independence, 445 U.S. 622 (1980)

        d. Municipalities are immune from punitive damages liability under Section 1983. City of Newport v. Fact Concerts, Inc., 453 U.S. 247 (1981)

        e. Attorney's fees awards are appropriate under Section 1988 even for nonconstitutional federal statutory violations, such as Social Security Act claims. Maher v. Gagne, 448 U.S. 122, 128 (1980)

    2. State Entities

a. The protection of the 11th Amendment does not
    extend generally to political subdivisions of
    the state, such as counties or municipalities.
    Lake Country Estates, Inc. v. Tahoe Regional
    Planning Agency, supra, stated the following
    test:

> By its terms, the protection afforded by
> that Amendment is only available to "one of
> the United States." It is true, of course,
> that some agencies exercising state power
> have been permitted to invoke the Amendment
> in order to protect the state treasury from
> liability that would have had essentially
> the same practical consequences as a
> judgment against the State itself. But the
> Court has consistently refused to construe
> the Amendment to afford protection to
> political subdivisions such as counties and
> municipalities, even though such entities
> exercise a "slice of state power." 440
> U.S. at 440-41.

b. The state's 11th Amendment protection extends
    not only to suits for damages but also to suits
    for injunctive relief that have a fiscal impact.
    Edelman v. Jordan, 415 U.S. 651 (1974), holds
    that the 11th Amendment precludes recovery of a
    money judgment against a state government even
    though the federal court judgment was in the
    form of an injunction requiring the payment of
    retroactive benefits to welfare recipients;
    however, the fiscal impact of an injunction
    prescribing prospective relief is not barred.

    (1) Hutto v. Finney, 437 U.S. 678 (1978), holds
         that an injunction against the state can be
         enforced through traditional contempt
         sanctions, such as civil fines, damages,
         and attorneys' fees, despite the fiscal
         impact on the state, as part of the
         prospective relief approved by Edelman.

171

(2) <u>Milliken</u> v. <u>Bradley</u>, 418 U.S. 717 (1974) and <u>Quern</u> v. <u>Jordan</u>, 440 U.S. 332 (1979) sustain certain remedial and ancillary types of relief that had fiscal impact on the state against an 11th Amendment challenge.

c. Congress has the power pursuant to Section 5 of the 14th Amendment to lift the 11th Amendment immunity of states.

(1) <u>Fitzpatrick</u> v. <u>Bitzer</u>, 427 U.S. 445 (1976), holds that Congress exercised this power when it extended Title VII's coverage and remedies to state governments in 1972, rendering states liable for back pay and attorneys' fees in employment discrimination cases.

(2) <u>Hutto</u> v. <u>Finney</u>, 437 U.S. at 693-94, holds that the Civil Rights Attorney's Fees Awards Act of 1976 was a second exercise of this power, rendering states liable for attorneys' fees awards to prevailing plaintiffs in Section 1983 cases.

(3) <u>Maher</u> v. <u>Gagne</u>, <u>supra</u>, holds that "Congress was acting within its enforcement power in allowing the award of fees in a case in which the plaintiff prevails on a wholly statutory, non-civil-rights claim pendent to a substantial constitutional claim or in one in which both a statutory and substantial constitutional claim are settled favorably to plaintiff without adjudication." 448 U.S. at 132

(4) <u>Quern</u> v. <u>Jordan</u>, 440 U.S. at 341, holds that Section 1983 did not lift the 11th Amendment immunity of states and that <u>Edelman</u> v. <u>Jordan</u> remains good law after <u>Monell</u> v. <u>Department of Social Services</u>.

C. Other Procedural Defenses

Both standing and abstention are important defenses commonly
raised in constitutional litigation, and the reader should
refer to the Rushing and Bratcher article for their treatment.
Important recent Section 1983 developments have occurred with
regard to statutes of limitations, exhaustion, and the
doctrines of res judicata and collateral estoppel.

1. Statutes and Limitations

    a. Board of Regents v. Tomanio, 446 U.S. 478 (1980),
        holds that the U.S. District Court hearing a Section
        1983 suit should apply both the analogous state
        statute of limitations to the plaintiff's federal
        constitutional claims and the state rules for tolling
        that statute of limitations.

    b. Garmon v. Foust, 668 F.2d 400 (8th Cir.) (en banc),
        cert. denied, 456 U.S. 998 (1982), holds that Section
        1983 claims will be governed by Iowa's general
        five-year statute of limitations, Iowa Code section
        614.1(4). The Court concluded that the 1983 cause of
        action for deprivation of civil rights in no way
        depends upon state common law and allows a litigant
        to pursue an action under statute rather than, or in
        addition to, state remedies. Consequently, the
        analogous Iowa statute of limitations for Section
        1983 claims is the general, catch-all statute of
        limitations, as Iowa has no specific period of
        limitations for actions based upon liability created
        by statute. Id. at 406 n. 11. The 8th Circuit did
        not consider the applicability of Iowa Code section
        613A.a, which requires any person claiming damages
        against a municipality to commence the action within
        six months of the incident (or, if the municipality
        receives written notice of the claim within six
        months of the incident, the plaintiff may commence
        the suit within two years of such notice). Id. at
        405 n. 9

c. Fourth Amendment Search and Seizure not limited to "tort" because it unduly cramps the significance of § 1983 as a broad statutory remedy.

d. Last term's Burnett decision.

2. Exhaustion of State Administrative Remedies

Patsy v. Board of Regents, 457 U.S. 496 (1982), unequivocally holds that exhaustion of state administrative remedies is not a prerequisite to bringing an action pursuant to Section 1983. Monroe re Judicial remedies (no exhaustion required). But see Agins v. City of Tiburon, 447 U.S. 255 (1980), not applicable where the use of state administrative remedies is necessary to create the unconstitutional taking (i.e, land use cases). Also Parratt, 451 U.S. 527 (1981), where postdeprivation remedy precluded a finding of a deprivation of property without procedural due process.

3. Res Judicata and Collateral Estoppel

a. Allen v. McCurry and Migra, holding that the doctrines of res judicata and collateral estoppel apply in civil rights actions under Section 1983, provided the state court was acting within its proper jurisdiction and the parties were afforded a "full and fair opportunity" to litigate federal claims.

b. Gear v. City of Des Moines, 514 F. Supp. 1218 (S.D. Iowa 1981), holds that the doctrine of collateral estoppel applied to state administrative contested case decisions under the Iowa Administrative Procedure Act and precluded relitigation of plaintiff's Section 1983 sex discrimination claim in federal court, even though the plaintiff did not seek judicial review of the agency decision in the state courts.

c. Kremer v. Chemical Construction Corp., 456 U.S. 461 (1982), holds that the federal court was required under 28 U.S.C. § 1738 to give preclusive effect to

174

the state-court decision upholding the state administrative agency's rejection of the employment discrimination claims. The case arose under Title VII, and the Court concluded that Title VII, like Section 1983, did not create an exception to Section 1738.

(1) Section 1738 requires federal courts to give the same preclusive effect to state court judgments that those judgments would be given in the courts of the states from which the judgments emerged. 456 U.S. at 465-66. The Court ruled that preclusive effect would be given the state court judgment, even though its review of the agency's factual determinations was under a substantial evidence scope of review. Id.

(2) Because Section 1738 is inappliable to state administrative determinations that have not been reviewed by state courts, Kremer confirmed "that initial resort to state administrative remedies does not deprive an individual of a right to a federal trial de novo on a Title VII claim." 456 U.S. at 477. "Since it is settled that decisions by the EEOC do not preclude a trial de novo in federal court, it is clear that unreviewed administrative determinations by state agencies also should not preclude such review even if such a decision were to be afforded preclusive effect in a state's own courts." 456 U.S. at 470 n. 7

(3) State judicial review of the state agency's adverse determination was sought by the complainant in Kremer, before he filed his Title VII suit in federal court. Kremer did not address the situation that arose in Gunther v. Iowa State Men's Reformatory, 612 F.2d 1079, 1084 (8th Cir.), cert. denied, 446 U.S. 966 (1980), where the complainant prevailed at the agency level and then had her adversary seek state judicial review. The Kremer dissent

points out the complainant could find herself
closed out of federal court if the state court
decides the agency's decision is unsupported by
sufficient evidence. 456 U.S. at 504 n. 18.
The 8th Circuit, which denied preclusive effect
to the state court decision, noted the
unfairness of applying preclusion where
plaintiff did not seek state court review but
was forced to defend by her adversary's appeal.
Gunther, 612 F.2d at 1805 n. 7

4. Abstention

   a. Younger Abstention

      Kaylor v. Fields, 661 F.2d 1177 (8th Cir. 1981)
      (Plaintiff sues prosecuting attorney to enjoin him
      from releasing information to the press. As to
      allegation that prosecuting attorney threatened to
      prosecute to punish for political beliefs, would not
      be enjoined because free speech is not a defense to a
      criminal prosecution.) (¶ C2) The test of Younger
      is:

      1. ongoing state judicial proceeding

      2. important state interests (criminal law,
         disciplinary proceedings for attorneys)

      3. adequate opportunity to present constitutional
         challenge.

   b. Pullman Abstention, 312 U.S. 496 (1941) (Unsettled
      issue of state law that would eliminate
      constitutional violation issue)

   c. Burford Abstention, 319 U.S. 315 (1943) (Complex
      state statutory scheme and comprehensive review
      procedures--if abstention furthers public policy and
      is in public interest)

176

IX. Exercise of the Police Power in the Land Use Context

A. Scope of the Police Power and How It Has Steadily Expanded to Include Various Land Use Regulations

1. Village of Euclid v. Ambler Realty Co., 272 U.S. 365 (1926) (The police power must expand to meet any different conditions in a changing world.)

2. Berman v. Parker, 348 U.S. 26 (1954) ("It is within the power of the legislature to determine that the community should be beautiful as well as healthy, spacious as well as clean, well-balanced as well as patrolled.")

3. Goldblatt v. Town of Hempstead, 369 U.S. 590 (1962) (public nuisance)

4. Golden v. Planning Board of the Town of Ramapo, 30 N.Y.2d 359, 285 N.E.2d 291, 334 N.Y.S.2d 138 (1972), appeal dismissed, 409 U.S. 1003 (1972) (growth management through timing and sequence controls)

5. Construction Industry Association v. City of Petaluma, 522 F.2d 897 (9th Cir. 1975), cert. denied, 424 U.S. 934 (city plan fixing yearly housing development growth rate)

6. Village of Belle Terre v. Boraas, 416 U.S. 1 (1974) (Village's restriction of land use to single-family dwellings upheld under the police power: "A quiet place where yards are wide, people few, and motor vehicles restricted are legitimate guidelines in a land-use project addressed to family needs.")

7. Just v. Marinette County, 201 N.W.2d 761 (Wis. 1972) (shoreline environmental zoning ordinance protecting navigability of state waters and recreational uses)

8. Penn Central Transportation Co. v. City of New York, 438 U.S. 104 (1978) (preservation of historic landmarks)

9. Metromedia, Inc. v. City of San Diego, 453 U.S. 490 (1981) (ordinance restricting billboards)

10. Holt Civic Club v. City of Tuscaloosa, 439 U.S. 60
(1978) (extension of police power to extraterritorial
communities upheld)

B. Limitations on the Scope of the Police Power and Doctrines That
Have Narrowed Its Exercise

1. Adherence to a Comprehensive Plan

a. Baker v. City of Milwaukee, 533 P.2d 772 (Or. 1975)
(Zoning decisions of a city must be in accord with
its comprehensive plan and any ordinance in conflict
must fail.)

b. Sabo v. Township of Monroe, 232 N.W.2d 584 (Mich.
1975) (Absence of plan will not necessarily
invalidate a zoning ordinance, but it will weaken the
presumption of validity.)

c. Forestview Homeowners Assoc., Inc. v. County of Cook,
390 N.E.2d 763 (Ill. 1974) (Absence of a plan may
lead to overturning the ordinance or weakening the
presumption of validity.)

2. Equal Protection, Racial Discrimination, and Exclusion

a. Park View Heights Corp. v. City of Black Jack, 605
F.2d 1033 (8th Cir. 1979), rev'd, 454 F. Supp. 1223
(E.D. Mo. 1978) (Where demise of racially integrated
town house development was a discriminatory effect of
violation of the Fair Housing Act in the form of a
discriminatory housing ordinance, intervening
economic factors were not sufficient to relieve city
of liability but were rather factors affecting
breadth of equitable relief.)

b. Village of Arlington Heights v. Metropolitan Housing
Development Corp., 429 U.S. 252 (1977)
(Developer/plaintiff failed to carry burden of
proving that refusal to rezone single- to multifamily
housing was motivated by discriminatory intent.
Discriminatory result is not enough; for violation of

equal protection, discriminatory intent must be shown.)

3. Regional General Welfare

    a.   Southern Burlington County NAACP v. Township of Mt. Laurel, 336 A.2d 713 (N.J.), cert. denied and appeal dismissed, 423 U.S. 808 (1975) (Ordinance making it physically and economically impossible to provide low- and moderate-income housing by large lot zoning, tax incentive, building size requirements, held invalid in that it failed to serve the general welfare.)

    b.   Township of Williston v. Chesterdale Farms, Inc., 341 A.2d 466 (Pa. 1975) (Zoning ordinance providing for apartment construction in only 80 of the 11,589 acres in township was unconstitutionally exclusionary.)

    c.   S.A.V.E. A Valuable Environment v. City of Bothell, 576 P.2d 401 (Wash. 1978) (City has a duty to serve welfare of entire affected community when acting on a rezone application where interest at stake is quality of environment.)

4. Takings, Inverse Condemnation, and Due Process

    a.   Pennsylvania Coal v. Mahon, 260 U.S. 393 (1922) (cited for Holmes's quote, "If regulation goes too far it will be recognized as a taking")

    b.   Hadachek v. Sebastian, 239 U.S. 394 (1915) (Diminution in value does not equal a taking. If regulation furthers the public welfare, a taking will be found only if the owner is left with no reasonable use.)

    c.   Eldridge v. City of Palo Alto, 57 Cal. App. 3d 613, 129 Cal. Rptr. 575 (1976) (Open space zoning is not in itself a taking but may be considered such if plaintiff can show acquisitory intent on the part of local government.)

d.   Penn Central Transportation Co. v. City of New York, 438 U.S. 104 (1978) (No taking where owner was able to transfer development rights of other property.)

e.   Agins v. City of Tiburon, 447 U.S. 255 (1980) (Under these facts, the Supreme Court refused to find a taking but indicated that injunctive and declaratory relief would be available for inverse condemnation under §1983.)

f.   Lake Country Estates, Inc. v. Tahoe Regional Planning Agency, 440 U.S. 391 (1979) (implies that damages are available under §1983 for inverse condemnation)

g.   San Diego Gas & Electric Co. v. City of San Diego, 450 U.S. 621 (1981) (Brennan's dissent, which included three others plus Rehnquist, who would have joined had he found there was a final judgment, would allow damages for temporary takings.)

X. Guidelines Concerning the Proprieties of Negotiations for Development Approval

A.   The ARRT Formula: Avoidance, Reduction, Retention, Transfer

1.   Avoidance: Avoidance of liability is obtained only by refusing to engage in the development approval process.

2.   Reduction of Risk

a.   Compliance with laws pertaining to conflicts of interest, sunshine laws, bidding, and the like

b.   Develop expertise; hire experts; special care for proprietary functions; serve the public health, welfare, and safety; keep records; perform audits; follow regulations; plan

3.   Despite avoidance and reduction, if liability results, who pays?

B.   Exercise of the Police Power in the Land Use Context Revisited

The proprieties of negotiations for development approval are best served if the rules laid down in Section IX, _supra_, are followed.

    a.   Retention: The   public   body   pays,   through self-insurance, risk pooling, or another means.

    b.   Transfer: The   primary   transfer   mechanism   is insurance. The coverages most needed are generally not available.

APPENDIX

Public Law 98-544
98th Congress

An Act

To clarify the application of the Clayton Act to the official conduct of local governments, and for other purposes.

Be it enacted by the Senate and House of Representatives of the United States of America in Congress assembled. That this Act may be cited as the "Local Government Antitrust Act of 1984".

SEC. 2.   For purposes of this Act--

(1) the term "local government" means--

(A) a city, county, parish, town, township, village, or any other general function governmental unit established by State law, or

(B) a school district, sanitary district, or any other special function governmental unit established by State law in one or more States,

(2) the term "person" has the meaning given it in subsection (a) of the first section of the Clayton Act (15 U.S.C. 12(A)), but does not include any local government as defined in paragraph (1) of this section, and

(3) the term "State" has the meaning given it in section 4C(2) of the Clayton Act (15 U.S.C. 15g(2)).

SEC. 3.   (a) No damages, interest on damages, costs, or attorney's fees may be recovered under section 4, 4A, or 4C of the Clayton Act (15 U.S.C. 15, 15a, or 15c) from any local government, or official or employee thereof acting in an official capacity.

(b) Subsection (a) shall not apply to cases commenced before the effective date of this Act unless the defendant established and the court determines, in light of all the circumstances, including the stage of litigation and the availability of alternative relief under the Clayton Act, that it would be inequitable not to apply this subsection to a pending case. In consideration of this section, existence of a jury verdict, district court judgment, or any stage of litigation subsequent thereto, shall be deemed to be prima facie evidence that subsection (a) shall not apply.

SEC. 4.   (a) No damages, interest on damages, costs, or attorney's fees may be recovered under section 4, 4A or 4C of the Clayton Act (15 U.S.C. 15, 15a, or 15c) in any claim against a person based on any official action directed by a local government, or official or employee thereof acting in an official capacity.

(b) Subsection (a) shall not apply with respect to cases commenced before the effective date of this Act.

SEC. 5.   Section 510 of the Department of Commerce, Justice, and State, the Judiciary, and Related Agencies Appropriation Act, 1985 (Public Law 98-411), is repealed.

SEC. 6.   This Act shall take effect thirty days before the date of the enactment of this Act.

Approved October 24, 1984.

Selected References

Claire, William H., III. "Winning through Negotiation." Planning (July/August 1983).

Cunningham and Kremer. "Vested Rights, Estoppel, and the Land Development Process." Hastings L.J. 29 (1978): 625, 629.

Fisher, Roger, and Ury, William. Getting to Yes: Negotiating Agreements without Giving In. Boston: Houghton Mifflin Company, 1981.

Frascogna, Xavier, Jr., and Hetherington, H. Lee. Negotiation Strategy for Lawyers. Englewood Cliffs, N. J.: Prentice-Hall, 1984.

Freilich, Robert, and Pal, Gene. New Developments in Land Use and Environmental Regulations. Institute on Planning, Zoning, and Eminent Domain, 1985.

Freilich, Robert, and Ragsdale, John. "Timing and Sequential Controls: The Essential Basis for Effective Regional Planning. An Analysis of the New Directions for Land Use Control in the Minneapolis-St. Paul Metropolitan Area." Minnesota Law Review 58 (1974): 1009.

Freilich, Robert, and Stuhler, Eric O. The Land Use Awakening: Zoning Law in the 70s. Chicago: ABA Press, 1981.

Hagman, Donald G. "Development Agreements." Zoning and Planning Law Report 3:10 (November 1980).

---. "Estoppel and Vesting in the Age of Multi-Land Use Permits." Southwestern University Law Review 11 (1979): 545.

Holliman, W.G. "Development Agreements and Vested Rights in California." Urban Lawyer 13:1 (Winter 1981).

Kirlin, John L., and Kirlin, Anne M. Public Choices--Private Resources: Financing Capital Infrastructure for California's Growth through Public-Private Bargaining. Sacramento, Calif.: California Tax Foundation, 1982.

Kramer. "Development Agreements: To What Extent Are They Enforceable?" Real Estate L.J. 10 (1981): 29, 45.

Levitt, Rachelle L., ed. Research Parks and Other Ventures: The University/Real Estate Connection. Washington, D.C.: ULI-the Urban Land Institute, 1985.

O'Hare, Michael; Bacow, Lawrence; and Sanderson, Debra. Facility Siting and Public Opposition. Chap. 6, "Negotiation." New York: Van Nostrand Reinhold, 1983.

Porter, Douglas; Phillips, Patrick; and Moore, Colleen. Working with the Community: A Development Guide. Washington, D.C.: ULI-the Urban Land Institute, 1985.

Quinn and Olstein. "Privatization: Public/Private Partnerships Providing Essential Services." Municipal Finance Journal 5 (1984): 247, 249.

Rushing and Bratcher. "Section 1983 Defenses." Urban Lawyer 14 (1982): 149.

Solnit, Albert. Project Approval: A Developer's Guide to Successful Local Government Review. Belmont, Calif.: Wadsworth Publishing Co., 1983.

Stout, Gary, and Vitt, Joseph. Public Incentives and Financing Techniques for Codevelopment. Washington, D.C.: ULI-the Urban Land Institute, 1982.

Sullivan, Timothy J. Resolving Development Disputes through Negotiations. New York: Plenum Press, 1984.

Talbot, Allan R. Settling Things: Six Case Studies in Environmental Mediation. Washington, D.C.: The Conservation Foundation, 1984.